D0787427

TRAVELS BY NIGHT

The author at twenty-one, sketched by Michael Behnan
(See Chapter Five)

TRAVELS BY NIGHT

A MEMOIR OF THE SIXTIES

DOUGLAS FETHERLING

LESTER
PUBLISHING

Canadian Cataloguing in Publication Data

Fetherling, Douglas, 1949–
Travels by night : a memoir of the sixties

ISBN 1-895555-66-3

1. Fetherling, Douglas, 1949–   . – Biography – Youth.
2. Canada – Intellectual life.
3. Authors, Canadian (English) – 20th century – Biography.*
I. Title.

PS8561.E34Z53   1994   C811'.54   C93-095520-X
PR9199.3.F48Z47   1994

Lester Publishing Limited
56 The Esplanade
Toronto, Ontario   M5E 1A7

Printed and bound in Canada
94 95 96 97 5 4 3 2 1

The Dreams of Ancient Peoples

Variorum: New Poems and Old 1965–1985

Moving towards the Vertical Horizon

Rites of Alienation

Chinese Anthology

The Blue Notebook: Reports on Canadian Culture

Notes from a Journal

The Five Lives of Ben Hecht

The Crowded Darkness

Some Day Soon: Essays on Canadian Songwriters

Year of the Horse: A Journey through Russia and China

Gold Diggers of 1929

The Gold Crusades:
A Social History of Gold Rushes 1849–1929

The Rise of the Canadian Newspaper

A Little Bit of Thunder

Week-in-Review

Documents in Canadian Art (editor)

CONTENTS

CHAPTER ONE

JOE FEATHERS AND THE DRAGON LADY

A LOVE OF SECRECY was the most obvious trait my parents had in common. I was thirty-five before I knew my mother's true age, forty before I learned where she was born. My father's name was George Fetherling, but he worked for years alongside people who believed he was Joe Feathers, as he had led them to infer. Instead of taking his children to the doctor's office when we had colds or other minor complaints, he would lead us to a hospital emergency room. That way he didn't have to give our real names. To his way of thinking, the privacy thus preserved more than made up for the greater expense and the long waits in tragic surroundings. Both he and my mother kept their finances secret from each other and from the world. They put the very few dollars they had in a number of widely scattered banks, which they would change frequently. They did so to prevent bank employees from spying on them.

Such people were naturally circumspect about their own families. If pressed they would sometimes allude to skeletons in closets. On examination most of these

embarrassments turned out to be small or long ago
neutralized by changes in society. Like the farm girl in a
thousand old ribald anecdotes, my maternal grandmother had become pregnant by a boarder. Two mar-
riages and seventy years later, only my mother continued
to be scandalized by the incident, which she would use
as a taunt. But the darkest secret in my family was secret
only in the sense that it was never mentioned. It didn't
have to be spoken of, because it was the most blatant and
pervasive and ultimately most damaging of all. It was the
sin of exogamy. My father was a product of the upper
middle class who through an unfortunate conjunction
of circumstance and personality married a lower-class
woman. The guilt he felt only increased her already considerable hostility and his own self-loathing. This, too,
sounds archaic, like the plot of a Victorian melodrama,
but the friction it produced was real enough to destroy
lives. Anger born of class tension became the dominant
element of my childhood.

The few records I have show that the Fetherlings
were steadily miscellaneous in character; in the standard
fashion of the nineteenth-century middle class, they
were farmers, teachers, soldiers and merchants, with
most of them having several such careers in sequence. It
was only with my grandfather, Herschel Fetherling,
whose life was divided in two by the turn of the century,
that the pattern was broken for better and for worse.
For reasons I have been unable to discover, a split in the
family caused some members to assume variant spel-
lings of the name. The schism, whatever it was, whether
political, financial or romantic, pitted my grandfather
against his brother Homer and may have pushed my

grandfather away from the pack. He was a graduate engineer but an entrepreneur by temperament and a quite civilized fellow to judge by such evidence as has survived. He died more than a decade before I was born, but in my distorted view, based on the stories I've heard and the artefacts I've seen, he had been many places and done many things.

As I write this I look at two photographs. One is a *carte de visite* from perhaps 1890, showing him posing in front of a screen painted with Corinthian columns. One arm and one scuffed boot rest with studied insouciance on a stump-like pillar. In his face I recognize my own features, the same nose, the same heavy eyebrows and slightly slanted eyes. Only the ears are different, and the lips, which are full, like my father's. He wears striped trousers and sports a silk bow tie below his winged collar. He stares into the lens, one hand languidly holding an unlighted cigarette, the other stuck in the pocket of his inverness. His derby is pushed back off his forehead. He looks as though he's pausing in his conquest of the world. The other portrait was taken to illustrate some magazine article he had written. It shows a thinner-faced man of mature years with white hair and wire spectacles, but the eyes are vulnerable and full of sorrow. By subtracting the one from the other, I get the sum of my father's early years.

My grandfather washed up in San Francisco at some point before the 1906 earthquake and fire. He was an enthusiastic photographer, and among bundles of old pictures I now wish someone had saved were studies he had made of Chinatown. I remember images of men hurrying along the street with their hands inserted in the ample sleeves of their robes and queues protruding from beneath their pillbox hats. Grandfather seems to have been a bit of an amateur orientalist in fact. He had spent a lot of time in the Chinese quarter and once narrowly escaped involvement in a tong war. One day he was strolling with a Chinese man, he on the side nearer the street, the Chinese on the other side, by a wooden hoarding. A highbinder suddenly popped up over the fence and implanted a small hatchet in the skull of the Chinese, who crumpled to the pavement. As he related the story to his son, Grandfather knew that the man had died instantly and that his own best hope lay in continuing the walk as though nothing had happened.

It was this period perhaps to which belonged some of the curios and *objets d'art* I recall seeing or being told about. The house I lived in as a boy was stuffed with dime-store kitsch such as matador statuettes and gaggles of plaster geese in flight. My mother's taste was thus a marked contrast to that represented by Grandfather's sets of standard authors, a model he had made of Henry Hudson's ship *Halfmoon*, his china and silver and dinner gong, and especially his orientalia, such as a set of bronze elephant figures, designed and cast with extraordinary skill and set on a four-foot teak base. He had a weakness for inexpensive Buddhas and lacquered cigarette boxes as well. At one time he had also collected murder weapons. He would prevail on certain policemen to sell these once their value in court had passed. One was a pepper-box revolver, its wooden grips eaten away, which had been dredged up from the bay. Another, likewise used in some grisly crime, was a three-foot triangular rasp or file, which the villain had ground on a wheel to make a three-sided sword with razor-sharp edges, then fitted with a bleached ham bone as a handle.

I have vivid memories of Ethel Jane Abbott, my paternal grandmother. She had been born in London and after some family set-backs, not excluding a cruel step-father, had managed to attend one of those European finishing schools that imbue their graduates with a particular sort of English joviality, a quality that becomes a lifelong hum, never varying in pitch. It was sometime before the First World War that she and Herschel settled in Pittsburgh, the base from which he travelled about, selling electrical equipment to industry as a rep of General Electric. The city was then in the glory of its decadent modernism but still dominated by Carnegies, Mellons and Fricks, indeed must have been very much the way the muckrakers had found it in the 1890s: a place where frivolous mansions went hand-in-hand with wretched immigrant slums, and pollution from the mills turned the streets dark by late morning or early afternoon. It was at some necessary level a city for making deals, and in that stratum Herschel prospered, as when he made a famous $4-million sale to Ernest T. Weir, the steel baron. Eventually he set up a company that sold mining machinery and the like (I'm looking at the logotype, a fancy winged F, which survives on a piece of his letterhead). He became a clubman and kept offices in Senator George T. Oliver's Chamber of Commerce Building, an opulent early skyscraper, and a small but pretty home in the Beltzhover district that he wired with a complicated private telephone exchange of his own devising. More than sixty years later, I saw the bedroom where my father was born in 1915, when his mother was thirty-three and his father was approaching fifty.

I've sometimes speculated about the atmosphere in which my father grew up. Certainly his home life was very English, for quite apart from the anglicisms in his speech that so annoyed my mother he had, I feel, an essentially English character, so rare in an American. He must have sensed that, without quite realizing what it was that made him so out of place. The U.S. coastal cities such as New York, San Francisco and even Los Angeles, and certainly including smaller ones such as Boston or New Orleans, are often open to civilizing influences, in part because clusters of exiles and expatriates keep alive the historic links those places have with other parts of the world, but the vast interior has always been dark and barbaric. I've come to suspect that this is partly what forced or permitted him to create an imaginative world for himself, a sort of shadow life, but one that never found proper expression and got subsumed in a general pattern of emotional self-destruction.

When as a boy I would go exploring in the cellar or cubby-hole attic, I would sometimes come upon a doll my father had played with so long ago; it was wooden, stuffed with sawdust, and named Jimmie McFadden. It's easy for me to visualize him carrying it about, or to see him in short trousers and a cloth cap, rolling a hoop or (another childish diversion of that place and time) chewing the hot tar with which the brick streets were repaired. The earliest memory he related to me dated back to the Great War. Near his home, some soldiers were being trained in the use of the new queer-looking vehicle called a tank, one of those small rhomboid ones with all the treads exposed. It was driven up a steep bank until it was in a vertical position, whereupon it rolled over on its back like a turtle. He also remembered hearing a postwar lecture by Sergeant Alvin York, the former conscientious objector from the Tennessee backwoods who became a national hero after abandoning his pacifism and capturing a company of Germans. When the Liberty Tubes, the tunnels connecting downtown Pittsburgh with the South Hills, were opened for traffic in the 1920s, Father and a playmate found a large wooden spool, the sort used for steel cable, on the hilltop hundreds of feet above. Thinking it would make a giant yo-yo, they wound a line around the shaft and, grasping the free end of the rope, rolled the toy off the edge. Fortunately they let go before the slack played out and carried them over the side. When it hit, the device narrowly missed someone's flivver. They had to flee to avoid apprehension.

The old city directories reveal that Herschel's father, Cephas Fetherling, a veteran of the War between the States, was part of the household for some of this time, and pension records tell the sad story of his life. He had enlisted in 1862, just before his eighteenth birthday, and less than a month later was captured by General Kirby Smith's Confederate cavalry and held as a prisoner-of-war in Richmond, though quickly paroled. He was promoted from private to commissary sergeant, then reduced to private again, and finally made commissary sergeant a second time. It was in that capacity that he was accused of selling army potatoes to a civilian. His file states that hard marching and exposure gave him lung fever and left him deaf in both ears, though despite the handicap he would become a teacher as well as a merchant. He was discharged at war's end by reason of chronic dysentery and in 1867 married one Sarah Hollinger. They were divorced in 1917, when they were both seventy-three, whereupon he quickly remarried. No doubt his presence had some bearing on his grandson even though the grandson was only two at the time of the divorce and only five when the old soldier died. The great stock crash, however, was the more important factor in my father's early development, the turning point of his life in fact, though he was only fourteen at the time.

Herschel must have been speculating heavily, for my father always spoke of October 1929 with the disbelieving humour that disguises genuine horror. When the panic solidified into the Depression, there was suddenly no money coming in, but my grandmother continued to operate on the same budget as before. Her expenditures included large bills for milk and cream, most of which went unused in a domestic economy that had suddenly contracted and no longer permitted entertaining. When Herschel received some cheque in the mail—in one telling, it was the last of his receivables—he handed it to her with the derisive suggestion that it was just about enough to pay the bill from the creamery.

It was my father's ill luck to graduate from high school in the dismal year 1933. Going on to university was now out of the question. I've always felt that this accident of timing, by preventing him from even becoming aware of a creative community, ensured that he never developed his large linguistic gift or his slightly smaller visual one and didn't become a writer or some variety of artist, as his sensibility as well as his talent would have suggested. He did try without success to get on at the *Post-Gazette* and perhaps other papers and then drifted for a while. He started working for his father, which must have been awkward charity, as Grandfather was soon reduced to such bizarre ventures as taking over a warehouse full of department store mannequins. When the possibility presented itself, Grandfather helped him find a job with General Electric. This proved a rare opportunity, and at length Father became a sort of supervisory mechanical trouble-shooter. When disaster struck, he would go off on short notice to some distant mill or power plant where company turbines had been installed. It meant working with his hands—at which he excelled—usually in unpleasant surroundings. On one occasion he nearly died of appendicitis in a hotel room in a town that had been evacuated while he'd slept. But there was a certain romance to it and romance was a quality he valued. He was proud of his knowledge of good restaurants and hotels throughout much of the East, though the most important compensation for such a nomadic bachelor life was that it preserved some sense of belonging to the middle class. He played golf, for example (judging by the set of clubs, including a huge polka-dotted niblick, which later mocked his loss of status from a dark corner of our cellar). Photographs of the period show a handsome fellow with thick black hair combed straight back and parted in the centre, well dressed in the 1930s manner, with expensive commodious suits and short silk neckties that hung down like elongated diamonds. He had been living that kind of life for five years when he met my mother, Mary Emma Jones.

The Joneses came from Glandyfi, a lead-mining town in Cardiganshire, not far from where the River Dovey enters the Bay of Cardigan, and my mother's father, Owen, stands out in my memory for his Welshness. He was a big man, not tall but barrel-chested, who recalled the likeness of Andrew Jackson on the American twenty-dollar bill, what with his huge stalk of white hair set off here and there by streaks of urinary yellow. He had come to rest in eastern Ohio, in the coal-mining and steel-making region that also includes the contiguous parts of West Virginia and Pennsylvania. At twelve, he had gone to work in the same steel-mill as his father, who dropped dead at his side, and at some point he had boxed in the Moscow Golden Gloves. Another time he took a raft down the Mississippi to New Orleans. Later still, when my mother was a girl, he ran a saloon— Coates & Jones Double Six, it was called; he may have won it at poker—and was also a salesman for Red Top beer, a vile brew. These enterprises were all in Martins Ferry, one of the small Ohio cities opposite Wheeling, West Virginia. I had grown up believing that my mother had been born in Canton, Ohio, somewhat farther west. Only after she died did the truth come out: she had been born in Martins Ferry but had chosen Canton because it sounded to her so much more cosmopolitan. It was at that time that I also learned she wasn't a high school graduate. In any case, by the late thirties, Grandfather Jones was a gruff, taciturn fellow who had had a lifetime's worth of different jobs. I see him in his singlet, sitting on the porch of his old farm-house (built over top of some early settler's log cabin), chewing Mail Pouch tobacco and staring out across the highway. Like Aldous Huxley, of whom he most assuredly never heard, he died on the day that President Kennedy was shot and was thus shortchanged in the amount of space the news of his passing was accorded in the papers.

————————

Following her encounter with the family's lodger, my maternal grandmother, Effie Lee Halm, who for some reason was always called Bill, married a man named Ogden. They had a son whom my mother, his half-sister, resented intensely, in part because he clawed his way into the bottom register of the middle class, as a small-time public relations man with a weekly news-paper column. If it was a characteristic of the Fether-lings to split into ever smaller factions and sever all contact, the Jones style was to continue to harass blood enemies down through the years (the exception involved my grandmother's sister, whom my mother wouldn't visit or speak to, though she spent her last four decades in a nursing home only a few miles away).

When Bill and Owen were wed in 1907, then, it was her second marriage. They had six daughters, of whom my mother, born in 1911, was the eldest but one. To reach their house, outside Martins Ferry, one crossed a small stream, called a run, by means of a bridge that Owen had made from utility poles he had appropriated for this pur-pose. They owned a cow and each spring got a pig and had an orchard that was slowly being reclaimed by the woods. But Owen kept selling off bits of land, to the point where it made sense to let the spring-house collapse and convert the barn into a house for one of my aunts.

This grandmother, whom I came to admire, was a small wiry woman with only a grade seven education but a good deal of common sense. She had a likeable manner and a natural gift for drawing, and she was never seen except in running shoes whose sides had split open, revealing ancient toes. After Owen died (they'd been together fifty-five years) she carried on much as before. One day when she was in her middle eighties, a caller arrived at dusk and, after searching the house in fear she'd suffered an accident, chanced to glance up towards the crest of a hill. He saw her silhouetted figure chopping down a tree with a double-bladed axe and chopping vigorously at that.

In trying to write of these matters, I may be reading too much into photographs, but such are the tools available. One snapshot of my mother, for instance, shows a young girl in flapper clothes standing in a patch of mud, trying to look urbane and urban, pursing her lips and feigning a kind of sophisticated disinterest. The image seems to me a revealing one. From her earliest period of consciousness, my mother disliked her life and surroundings but lacked any means of improving or changing them, was bound to them, in fact, by the twists and turns of her personality. She had no patience for anything rural, including her parents and siblings. It must have been a special kind of torture for her to be a teenager in the Roaring Twenties, yearning to be part of

Flaming Youth but knowing that, though the popular culture found its way even to the hills behind Martins Ferry, there was no possibility that she could be a part of what it represented. So as soon as she could, she left home and got a job. First she worked in a printing shop in the Ferry and then made what seemed the big move to Columbus, the state capital, 150 miles away. Forever afterwards she would speak of Columbus, Ohio, as though it were Paris or Rio, much to the embarrassment or hilarity of others even a little more worldly. But she was apparently not wholly successful there.

In 1938 when she met my father, she was already twenty-seven and living back at the hated farmhouse with her parents and sisters. Though her manner wasn't suited to dealing with the public, she was working as a hostess at a restaurant in Wheeling when my vagabond father came in for lunch with some business associates. She was short and buxom with Rita Hayworth hair (the testimony of the camera once again). He looked a little like Dick Powell, whom he confused with another actor, William Powell, and so claimed to have known when the latter was a movie usher in Pittsburgh. She seemed to promise the anonymity he was seeking, the totally workaday world that would offer no reminders of what he was because it brooked no comparison with what he might have been. From her point of view, he was her ticket to the bright lights. Their expectations contradicted each other. The resulting disaster went on for more than twenty-five years.

My mother must have enjoyed the first leg of their marriage, when they would live for extended periods in apartment-hotels in places such as Philadelphia, but in time she must have come to dread the prospect of packing up and moving on. Father was still only in his mid-twenties but was perhaps starting to weary of the work in any case, particularly as he was having difficulty with one of his bosses at the head office, an old enemy of his father's. I suspect that Mother was urging him to resign. In 1941 he was attached to some company project in Baltimore when their first child, my brother Dale, was born. The Second World War was being fought, still without U.S. participation, and some of the merchant ships they saw in the harbour had huge American flags, two or three hundred feet long, painted on them, so that U-boat commanders in the North Atlantic wouldn't mistake them for British. An old letter I found after her death tells me that when war finally came she was holed up with the three-month-old baby at her parents' farmhouse while her husband continued to travel on assignments. In the letter, Father describes driving eastwards over the Allegheny Mountains late at night and putting up at Cumberland, Maryland. "When I arrived here the folk with whom I room invited me to have a cup of coffee and a piece of cake and we sat and talked and listened to the radio. I wonder if the United States is going to declare war on Japan now after what happened today?" Pearl Harbor.

I can only speculate on what besides his wife's urging made him quit the job. He may have been worried about being drafted, as what he was doing was by no means the sort of essential work for which he might get a deferment. In any event, he finally ignored an order to hurry off to some new assignment and was long gone in another direction before the telegram from his nemesis, telling him he was fired, caught up with him. He went to Martins Ferry where Owen, who had been taken on as a security guard at a machine-tool plant and foundry, suggested that he apply for work at the company's other facility, across the river in Wheeling. The firm had recently retooled for defence contracting and so promised draft exemptions for employees. When my father turned up, a surly personnel manager asked if he was enough of a machinist to make a wristwatch if called on to do so. To this idiotic question he replied yes of course and was soon foreman of a crew of women who assembled anti-aircraft guns for the navy. My brother would say that the ones aboard the ship he served on during the Vietnam War were very likely made there at that time.

Father used to hypothesize that if the war had continued he might have become a success (in spite of himself). As it was, when the troops returned he ceased being a supervisor and lapsed into being a mere machinist and never again had any money beyond what immediate necessities called for. He drove wreck automobiles that were fifteen years old or more, so old that even other workingmen mocked him as he kept them alive season after season by mechanical ability alone. The marriage started to come undone. Reading the letters they exchanged when the times were fat and they were apart, I find no trace of the couple I knew when times were hard and they were together. Whatever flicker of love they might have had in the rapture of convenience faded quickly. It could never reignite, given my mother's steep decline into mental illness, alcoholism and abusive behaviour.

They lived at this time in an apartment on Wheeling Island, within easy sight of the massive cables and deck of the Wheeling Suspension Bridge, which was the longest one in the world when it was built in the 1840s and which throws the same sort of shadow over the Island that its descendant, the Brooklyn Bridge, casts over Brooklyn. Almost every spring, with the Ohio in flood, they would move their possessions to the top floor and sit without heat or electricity as the filthy water climbed the stairs like a heavy policeman and sloshed inside the walls. On one such occasion my father was rowing a punt through the streets helping others, and he picked up a drunk who insisted on standing in the boat. When they struck a submerged stop sign, the passenger fell overboard. Father dived in to save him, which he did without difficulty, but he got separated from the boat and had to make for a ledge on the second storey of a nearby building. When, some-time later, the authorities discovered his empty boat snagged on an obstruction downstream, he was reported missing, and the news found its way onto the radio, to the great anxiety of his friends.

After my brother, there was a second baby, born dead, and I suspect that the marriage already had deteri-orated into psychotic combat by the time of the third and no doubt unwanted pregnancy, which resulted in my birth in 1949. The expectation of another child drove them to look for more space, which they found a mile or two outside the city. Their discovery was a homemade four-room structure in Bethlehem, a little village of nondescript houses and even a few old farms, strung along two paved roads that came together in a general store and terminated in tough road-houses at either end. The owner was in difficulty with the law and wanted only $5,000, a sum it took my father about fifteen years to pay off. The lot sloped down to the woods and was flanked by open fields. Along the frontage stood a wide hedge through which speeding cars sometimes crashed en route to one of the notorious road-houses, a place called the Hi-Up. The village constable was an ex-convict who, my brother recalls, used to stop by the local school and let the kids play with his service revolver during recess; later, he changed careers and bought the Hi-Up, where he was beaten to death with a lead pipe.

Like West Virginia as a whole perhaps, Bethlehem combined the worst of the city with the worst of the countryside. The problem was the goddam trees, my mother would say almost nightly. "I look out these windows all day and all I can see is them goddam trees."

———————

One of the most curious aspects of childhood is the ability to accept grotesque surroundings as though they are perfectly normal. Having no basis for comparison, no yardstick of reality, the child believes that whatever's familiar must also therefore be ordinary and proper. Such was the case for me in the early 1950s. My first spurt of growth in other than the purely physical sense was the realization of just how freakish the little world my parents had made for themselves really was. The discovery was both frightening and unbearably sad.

In the late autumn or winter, when the goddam trees

were bare, you could get a wide-angle view of Wheeling from the top of Suicide: Suicide Hill, a mountain road that connected the city to the village. Wheeling was urban. Bethlehem was not, though it was quickly becoming one of Wheeling's bedroom communities. It was popular, for instance, with members of the mob that controlled Wheeling's criminal life, which was one of the city's big attractions to visitors and an important factor in the economy. But ordinary middle-class people were moving in as well, steadily filling up the spaces between the older houses. My mother got on with them even less well than she did with the locals of more or less her own background, who were more inclined to accept her tales of the fabled riches of Columbus. Her hobby was litigation, thanks in part, I believe, to questionable lawyers who took on her suits without a retainer, in the expectation of getting most of the settlement, and she would sometimes threaten action against some of the neighbours with whom, in any event, she feuded for years on end.

Another means of egress, when the soft sandstone cliffs gave way and Suicide was closed by slides, was an unpaved road called the Hollow. It began in a wooded area near our place and ended far below in the grit of 29th Street, Wheeling. Along the way lived families in one- and two-room shacks, supported—like the rusting hulks of cars out front—on four concrete blocks. Dirty-faced kids in torn clothes played in a little stream that carried away sewage, and emaciated, flea-bitten dogs, often with open wounds or terrible growths, were chained to trees and barked maniacally. The other extreme was perhaps no more than half a mile away and included several mysterious residents who were accused of being millionaires, such as Herman Strauss, who owned a junkyard. But even they were easily dominated, as we all were, by the figure of Carl Bachmann, whose large house looked down on the rest of the village from atop a private hill, protected by flood lights and a security network of trees and accessible only by private road. Bachmann was a retired politician, whom Edmund Wilson, writing during the Depression, had called "the caricaturist's ideal of the lower order of congressman... pot-gutted and greasy-looking, with small black pig-like eyes and a long pointed nose." So vast were his holdings in real estate, built up during the thirties, that in conversation he was presumed to be the owner of any land not obviously held by someone else. The village was thus a sort of socio-economic ant farm that any student of abnormality could have studied with profit.

A few houses west was a family I'll call Neuhardt and a few doors to the east of us lived their cousins, who had changed the spelling to Newhart once the head of the household got out of penitentiary. The Newharts had a mentally handicapped son who was left physically handicapped as well, in the polio epidemics of the early 1950s. He was four or five years older than I was but in the same grade at school, and would walk on crutches up and down all Bachmann's sad wooded hills wearing a big sheath knife and carrying a bow and arrow, with his collie playing at his heels. One day he butchered the dog with the knife and strung its intestines from the trees, and we never saw the boy again after that.

The other branch of the family, the unreconstructed Neuhardts, lived in a square insulbrick farmhouse from perhaps the 1870s. The father was a janitor at one of the steel plants and had elected not to accept promotion to another almost equally menial job because, he said, he couldn't deal with the increased responsibility. Then he got laid off and through careful manipulation was able to remain laid off for two years or so. Returning from some tavern late one night, he put his car in the claptrap garage and in closing the overhead door in the dark managed to lodge his thumb in the sash and so suspend himself off the ground. Whether from stoicism or an uncomplicated nature, he refused to call out and was found hours later, unconscious and weak from loss of blood, by his anxious wife. Her name was Dot and she was one of a vast network of inconspicuous women who supported their families making punch-boards for the Wheeling mob, which installed them and other crude gaming devices in every bar and beer-joint. Their daughter married a hillbilly in an elaborate ceremony and moved into a trailer on her new father-in-law's farm, where the bridegroom worked for five dollars a week, his only income.

For a period of several seasons between decades of ill will or silence, my mother had Dot as perhaps her only friend in the village, and it was during this interval that Dot's father-in-law, a recluse who inhabited a cabin-like structure in the woods behind our home, died. For years, Dot had been his only visitor, walking down the ravine along the fetid stream to bring him food. At length she persuaded him to have a telephone, but the calls she made to check up on him were the only occasions the instrument was used, because he didn't know how to dial. It was said that he was a crazy inventor and spent much of his time trying unsuccessfully to obtain patents on various children's games he'd devised. One night I was awakened by the unanimous baying of all the local dogs. Old Man Neuhardt had died and the animals, sensing death, circled the cabin and howled at the moon. Once the body was taken away, Dot, my mother and I went through the fellow's personal effects. They consisted mainly of bent tin cups, cracked dinner plates, the clothes of his long-dead wife, a regimental photograph from the First World War and dusty pieces of kids' games, with moveable squares and boards that were supposed to light up but didn't. Later, the fire department, needing practice, set the house ablaze with kerosene and let it burn to the foundation before trying to extinguish the flames at the last moment, when there was danger of igniting the tall grass and weeds and even the elms and maple poplars, which grew thickly over that part of the country. I can still see the firemen enjoying themselves, their faces distorted through the flames.

I ran away for the first time when I was about three. I had gone only a few hundred yards before being spotted by another of the local characters, a middle-aged woman named Myrtle who spent her days walking up and down the roadside pulling a child's red wagon, always empty. When I reached school age I might have found a more successful type of escape, but didn't. We were far from being one of the poor families—kids from the Hollow would turn up coatless and sockless in winter—but of the others, we were the shabbiest. My

mother would often buy us secondhand clothes at the
Wheeling Symphony Society Thrift Store; she tended
to grab whatever she saw and so I sometimes got girls'
tops rather than boys' shirts, with the buttons on the
left-hand side, and my brother remembers wearing gar-
ments that still had the names of his friends' fathers
sewn inside.

The other problem was that I stuttered so badly as to
barely speak at all. Asked my name, for instance, I
would strain and sputter and turn red, trying to flick
the words off the end of my wet tongue until it was sore
at the roots. On really bad days, when the veins in my
neck were distended as I tried to speak, I'd end up snapping my fingers or even flapping my arms like a big
flightless bird, trying to make a rhythm on which I
could get started. Most of the teachers were under-
standably exasperated and, what with their relative lack
of training, often questioned whether I was of normal
intelligence. One year I was actually kept from moving
on to the next grade on the grounds that I was slow, as
people said in those days. I withdrew further and further, and there were long spells when I dreaded both
going to school and coming home afterwards.

My father got up at 5:30 each morning to leave for
the plant and make machines used in making other
machines, and he didn't return for twelve hours. He
took whatever overtime was offered, to compensate for
frequent lay-offs and strikes, and so there were periods
when he would work seven days a week. In winter, that
meant he wouldn't see daylight for long stretches.
Through it all he remained convivial to the point of
being jolly, patient to the point of being weak. He

would sing "I'm a Ding-dong Daddy from Doomas" and "It Ain't No Sin to Take Off Your Skin (And Dance Around in Your Bones)," songs that scarcely anyone else his own age seemed to remember. The people he worked with all liked him whether or not they respected him, for while his stories of the outside world, told in richly coloured language, were always entertaining, he couldn't help standing slightly apart if for no other reason than that he was more articulate than they were.

Although he was passionate in his desire to see the worker get a square deal, he was ashamed to carry a metal lunch bucket, taking a paper bag instead so that he could dispose of the evidence at the end of each day. Similarly, although he wore old trousers and a type of flannel shirt then associated with labourers, he was always careful that they were spotless and in good repair, not greasy, smudged and torn like the other men's. I remember once being in a shop with him, inspecting some small piece of merchandise, a wristwatch perhaps, when the clerk noticed the rough worn skin of his hands and in condescending fashion guessed that he must work outdoors, as a contractor perhaps. I could see my father was embarrassed and angry, but he said, yes, a contractor, that's right, and we stayed just long enough looking at the watch to make a retreat seem natural. He tried mightily to lose himself in the world his dereliction had made him heir to, but there were always tiny signs of a struggle never to be resolved.

There were a few co-workers whom he saw outside the plant. One was Louie the Welder, who was actually a blacksmith. Another was a man whose shotgun had discharged, taking off his left foot, as he climbed a rail fence during a hunting trip. At the time, his handicap had been useful in keeping him out of the army, but now he was embarrassed by it. So he disguised his limp by always carrying a heavy box of television tubes wherever he went, implying that he was a qualified repairman. Father's closest friend was a large fellow he called Alec who had five or six children who thought he was a drunk and lived across the river, on the Ohio side, in a rickety house that seemed in danger of sliding down the hill in the spring mud and settling in one of the craters left by strip-mining. Father and he would sometimes drink together in a beer-joint where the barmaid was known as Thundergut, owing to a loud intestinal complaint from which she suffered. My mother never shared his affection for such people or for people in general and would become downright venomous if anyone made a claim on his attention.

She would have a head start on the night's drinking by the time he returned from work each day. In addition to knocking off six or eight beers, she would swig from the bottles of bourbon or Canadian whisky kept in the cigarette-burned sideboard. Such prodigious consumption of alcohol did nothing to increase her tolerance for it or improve her outlook. Far from making her maudlin, it activated her bile. By mid-afternoon she would be feeling pretty antagonistic towards the world, though sometimes I would empty out some of the whisky and replace it with water. By the end of the day she was lying in wait, ready to lash out at everyone in sight in the cruellest, most vituperative manner of which her vocabulary was capable. Her eyes would narrow, her face would become contorted and even her voice seemed to change, taking on a guttural unmodulated tone that was made even more otherworldly by the sharpness of her words.

Father would sit down at the kitchen table, under the cheesecake calendar from Levin Auto Parts. She would look peeved. He would ask what the matter was and get no response. Then it would begin.

"Money," she'd say, spitting out the word. "You haven't saved a goddam cent the whole time."

He'd tell her again that he was trying to better himself, working up through the ranks of the union, the only course open to a man without education. He couldn't go on all his life working in a foundry, he would say. "I'm not that young anymore." She'd snort contemptuously. "You don't fool me, running round with them bums!" She was a chain-smoker and had a tendency to chew the end of her unfiltered cigarette, which soon became a sodden mess; wet tobacco would swim out one corner of her mouth as she spoke.

Father would say he was doing it all for her, but he spoke without much conviction. As the fight reached a high pitch, it became increasingly one-sided, with Father staying quiet for the most part, giving the impression of someone who wanted only to lie down.

"What have I done to provoke your wrath?" he would ask.

That choice of words was always enough to send her off in new paroxysms of anger.

By this time, dinner would be under way, something taken from a can and heated or fried in a skillet, though on one occasion I remember vividly an enormous bowl of spaghetti. She raised it over her head and threw it at us, sending noodles everywhere and giving us a coating of tomato sauce that looked like blood. Such violent behaviour was not an occasional thing; it was the daily stuff of life. I remember sobbing spasmodically after being hit. I remember even more clearly how my brother, who by then was taller than she was, simply put up his palms and easily stopped her from hitting him: that really made her mad.

God help me, I'm trying not to recall her in too harsh a light, knowing that her alcoholism masked whatever lay underneath and that, in any event, she was merely exercising the only power she had, the power to make others pay attention to her by raving at them. Yet even now I marvel at the level of destructiveness as well as the crudeness of her emotions. The truth was that her life was drab and meaningless. Giving vent to her hatred seemed the only way she knew to relieve the monotony, though the rage itself became monotonous and could only be alleviated by committing even more emotional vandalism.

———————

By any customary standard of measure, she wasn't a bright woman—just bright enough to know that everyone else seemed smarter, which only heightened her frustration and sense of inferiority. The fact that she wasn't qualified to drive a car played some part in the social claustrophobia she suffered, and she would take or make any opportunity to get away from home for a few hours. For instance, she would drag my father off to funeral homes to view the remains of the most tenuous acquaintances or sometimes, I suspect, those of people she had never met at all. I was expected to be standing at the ready inside the door when they came home, asking "How did he look?" or "How did she look?" with a solemnity I really didn't understand. She would then review the undertaker's handiwork, praising some aspects of it, finding fault with others.

Or she would pretend to have heard a hurricane warning on the radio and insist on being taken to some restaurant in Wheeling, proceeding on the rule, known only to her, that in hurricanes, unlike floods, the low-lying areas are safer than the higher elevations. On rare occasions, this tactic would result in a meal at one of the big round tables at Billy's Spaghetti House, an establishment that Big Bill Lias, the local crime lord, ran in Centre Wheeling (a part of town whose spelling—Centre, not Center—so unusual in America, gives some indication of its age). Most commonly, however, it meant going to Pete & Marie's, a greasy spoon and beer-joint whose front room, where we sat, had display cases full of fishing tackle. These nights out, however, couldn't be depended on to improve her mood, and I came to dread them horribly. At home I could at least hide out of sight if not out of earshot. At Pete & Marie's I was stuck at the same table as my parents as Mother yelled and argued, sometimes attracting attention from the rummies, the welfare families and the occasional hooker who frequented the place. Either because he wanted only peace and quiet or perhaps because he could see her personality deteriorating, Father would seldom speak unkindly *to* her or even *of* her. The harshest comment he would allow himself, and it was used out of her hearing, was a reference to "the Dragon Lady," the name of an Asian virago in the comic strip "Terry and the Pirates."

Another crisis was building in the family at this time. Young as I was, I believe I understood.

When my grandfather Herschel died in 1938, Grandmother Fetherling's finances declined to levels undreamed of even in the Depression. She put the family home on the market. Later I learned that she risked calumny and worse to sell it to a Black family, the first such transaction in what's now almost entirely an African-American area. The money must have gone quickly, for by 1943, judging from the Pittsburgh city directory, she was employed in the laundry of the William Penn Hotel. This can't have been ennobling work for a woman of her background, but she stayed at it throughout her sixties and into her early seventies until in 1954 she came to live with us, over my mother's violent objections.

We rented a small trailer and returned from Pittsburgh in a torrential rain with her belongings. She had lived there in a slum in Carson Street, opposite the Jones & Laughlin steel-mill, whose black and orange discharge covered the neighbourhood with poisonous residue. The mementos of her better days filled every corner of her apartment, and made quite a load. Once Grandmother had settled in with us, Mother was full of derision for these "antiques," a term she imbued with special contempt, and began selling them to dealers who, predictably, she ever afterwards insisted had robbed her blind. Grandmother would sometimes spend time reading books, a practice Mother found infuriating in anyone, particularly her mother-in-law.

They would have long and complicated arguments, or rather, Mother would argue and Grandmother would reply with bewildered moderation, addressing her antagonist as *Dear*.

There were only two bedrooms in the house and Grandmother had to share the smaller one with my brother and me. She slept on a cot placed lengthwise at the bottom of our two beds. There was little privacy. The door to my parents' bedroom was a secondhand one from an old hotel—the number *10* was still visible beneath many layers of paint—but Mother would never allow us to have a door of any sort on ours.

One day I entered the house and heard the two women having the worst one-sided argument yet. Mother was screaming, strutting, banging blindly into furniture. The veins in her forehead were enlarged and pulsating, and I feared the violence might escalate. It was a terrible scene to happen on, like a rape or a battle. The real adversary, of course, was my father, and he lost. Soon Grandmother returned to Pittsburgh and far greater poverty, where as far as I know he contrived to visit her only once or twice, so great being my mother's dislike of her and so worn down had he become by years of his wife's behaviour. I confess that when I succeeded my father I showed no more moral courage than he had displayed in the circumstances. But when, later in the 1960s, Grandmother died in the charity ward of a Pittsburgh hospital, I did argue for saving her from potter's field, and her body was brought to Wheeling where Mother and I sat alone in the funeral home in front of the coffin. Whatever acquaintances she had made in Wheeling during her short stay had predeceased her.

Whatever friends of my father's might otherwise have come stayed away lest they meet my mother. I wanted to have a tombstone put up but Mother wouldn't hear of it.

One of Mother's rhetorical devices was to pinpoint her own shortcomings and attribute them to others. For example, she was more than once banished from a local beer-joint after waddling up to one of the other patrons and drunkenly calling him a lush. In that same spirit she would sometimes accuse Father of being a secret gambler. The charge was laughable, given not only his conservatism about money but also the fact that, for one period of a few years, her own gambling was quite out of control. It led to the only occasion I can recall on which Father took decisive retaliatory action or pretended to.

When I was a small boy she would put on one of her good dresses left over from the Second World War and take me with her to Wheeling Downs, the Island racetrack that Big Bill Lias operated. Lias, who weighed 350 pounds, had started out driving a bread wagon through South Wheeling, a dark labyrinth of narrow brick streets, Polish slums and evanescent factories. It was the last job he ever held free of annoying legal ambiguities. With Prohibition he became a famous bootlegger, then the king of the numbers racket, then proprietor of a string of night-clubs and casinos. He employed a hundred armed men but his payroll was much bigger than that suggests, what with cops, judges, congressmen and the like.

The federal authorities were forever trying to deport him, contending that he'd been born in Greece (his full name was Liakakos), not in South Wheeling. They did manage to convict him of income tax evasion and seize his known assets, including Wheeling Downs. But then, finding themselves with a race-track on their hands, they hired him to run it, an arrangement that broke as a scandal when it was revealed that Big Bill was the third-highest-paid federal employee, close behind the president and the chief justice of the supreme court. I would always be dragged to the Downs somewhat against my will, as I would be dragged other days to the various bookie joints, including one located in the back room of a candy store on Market Street and another whose front was a milliner's shop. Between the bookies and the pari-mutuel window, Mother was losing a hundred dollars a week, which was rather more than my father earned. The hot walker at the track, incidentally, was Charles Manson. Many years later, when lodged in San Quentin for the Tate-LaBianca murders of the 1960s, he would wax nostalgic in the press about his days working for Big Bill at the Downs. He even wrote to the warden of the West Virginia Penitentiary, a few miles from his old haunt, asking if he might be allowed to serve the rest of his life sentences in the same institution where his mother and several other members of his family had done time. The Mansons were excitable people.

It was some while before the worst of Mother's gambling streak ran its course and she relaxed to the point of phoning penny-ante bets to a Centre Wheeling saloon-keeper who made a little book on the side. One day she placed a wager on a rather far-fetched daily double and forgot about it until the late afternoon when she heard the results on the radio and realized that both her long shots had come in. The combination paid several hundred dollars. She immediately called the bookie, who tried to weasel out, saying that he'd forgotten to give it to the runner but would gladly refund her couple of bucks.

She worked herself into an incoherent rage that found its target in my father as soon as he got home from work. After a while he was unable to stand her harangue any longer and went upstairs to a chest-high attic off their bedroom. From its hiding place under the eaves, he extracted the .32 calibre revolver that his father-in-law had carried as a security guard to deter Nazi saboteurs. I must have been eight or nine at the time. I remember that he stuck me in the back seat of the 1949 Ford, which had an elasticised safety rope across the rear of the front seat, which I used as the reins of an imaginary stagecoach and bounced along merrily. It was a summer night shortly after dusk. We drove to a section of run-down Victorian row-houses and decrepit mansions now broken up into furnished rooms. He told me to be quiet, and taking the pistol with him he walked across the street to the saloon-keeper's house.

The buildings in the row were dark except the one my father headed for. Through the open front door, I could see a man's bare feet protruding over the end of a sofa and, some distance away, a square of white light from a television screen. Father looked around him and entered the house. The feet jumped to the floor, making a whole man, wearing an undershirt, come into view. Father closed the door behind him and all I could see was a thin rectangle of light around the edges. There were no shots and I never knew what happened. I'm inclined to believe that Father came away with the money we were owed, but my brother, who's older and therefore knew him longer than I did, feels just the opposite.

———————

Looking back I realize how unhealthy we were. We tended to have bad teeth, for instance, owing to poor care as much as to diet, for the family dentist was an alcoholic. He did little if any work on the patients who came to his office on Market Street and that was just as well. To steady his nerves he found it necessary to disappear frequently into the small adjoining room in which X-rays were developed, emerging with the sickly sweet smell of booze on his breath, his hand no steadier than before. On one occasion he drilled a tooth of mine left-handed. His right, which he normally used, was incapacitated by terrible burns. He had been in an accident with a steam pipe in the laundry of the state mental hospital at Weston in Lewis County.

As for my mother, her vision was poor but she refused to be fitted with proper glasses and instead bought plastic ones at the dime store, thus causing my father to make reference to "the family optician, Dr. Kresge." Of these play-spectacles she had several pair at a time, since in her near-sightedness she was always misplacing them and so required a second pair to locate the first. She wore them suspended from a chain, but would invariably lose that, too, when one of the arms broke off despite the surgical tape and band-aids used to repair it.

When found, the glasses would be filthy with spilt beer and spittle and the loose tobacco from broken cigarettes at the bottom of her handbag. Wiping the specs on her clothes perfunctorily, she would seat herself in front of the television for an evening's entertainment. But she would always find it difficult to concentrate on the plays, as she called all television programmes. "They've just got too many characters in 'em as far as I'm concerned," she'd say. And so it was that she would enlist Father in the nightly visit to 29th Street.

In my *patrie intérieure*, 29th Street is marked indelibly. It was long, wide, low and grey, the line dividing Centre Wheeling from South Wheeling. Centre Wheeling was a strangely comforting place, the site of, for instance, the barber shop my father patronized. The proprietor was a self-ordained minister who would sometimes preach at his customers, snipping and sermonizing interchangeably. He was, I think now, not quite sane, but I liked going there because there were stuffed lizards all over the shop, hanging from the walls and lurking behind the tall glass jars of pale blue disinfectant. Centre Wheeling was a decaying German neighbourhood, much of it built in the 1850s, and it was full of interesting spots such as this. I would sometimes walk through St. Alphonsus parish and see people at dinner safe inside their dirty brick houses and I would envy Roman Catholics their sense of family. Like my secret adolescent longings for the friendship of these family's daughters—all those loving and lovely Anne Maries and Mary Margarets—this was a heresy I kept to myself. South Wheeling was entirely different: menacing and rank. The Angel of Death had a summer place there.

There were elements of both districts in 29th Street where my parents would spend four or five hours each night drinking at a beer-joint called the Top Hat. Occasionally I could persuade them to leave me at home and would sometimes feign illness in order to avoid going. But that meant only that I would worry more as time passed until, finally, their 1951 Mercury (successor to the Ford) pulled up the road. As often as not, though, they would remain seated in the car for perhaps half an hour before entering the house. I could see them through the window, she arguing, gesticulating wildly, while he did nothing in particular. I knew the quarrel that never quite died out had gained new momentum. Soon she'd be stalking through the house, sulking for a bit, then flaring up volcanically amid breaking dishes and general household damage. In the event, it was no better being at home than it was going to the Top Hat.

Mother preferred to enter the Hat by its side door ("Ladies and Escorts"), as though that somehow made the interior better. The place was one enormous room with a low ceiling of pressed tin. A tongue-and-groove partition ran half the length, separating the bar itself from a dark area with wooden tables scattered helter-skelter. At the far end stood a small stage. According to legend, Helen Morgan, the singer of the 1920s, had once performed there in her early days, but no one had used it in years, perhaps decades, and the piano was covered in dust. There was a trap door in the floor, giving access to an underground run where beer-kegs could be cooled if one wasn't afraid of rats. The men's room had a swinging door and the whole place stank of backed-up urinals.

There were spittoons at either end of the bar, behind which, amid the point-of-sale ads for Duquesne, Pabst's Blue Ribbon and Iron City, was the imperturbable figure of Nick, the owner, who dried the drinking glasses on his apron. He was a Pittsburgh boy like my father, a few years younger but close enough so that their nostalgias overlapped. Opposite the bar was a Budweiser ad featuring a print of *Custer's Last Stand* by Cassily Adams, a painting in which Custer's long hair flowed magnificently as he withstood the inevitable slaughter—at the hands of Indians carrying African shields. Below this was a table at which a poker game was always in progress, under an adjustable green-shaded light. One night a man who had joined the game was sitting with his back to someone at the bar with whom he had been having an argument over fifty cents. It was Thursday, pay day at the plants, and a modest spread of cold cuts and pigs' knuckles lay at the far end of the bar. The man not in the game returned from the free lunch with a fork and stuck it in the skull of the poker player, who collapsed bleeding amid cards and chips and was carried off to the toilet by his friends. The attacker finished his beer and left.

In that era it was illegal in West Virginia to sell or consume liquor by the glass, even in hotels and restaurants, but all of the beer-joints freely offered thirty-five-cent shots as the natural antidote to their twenty-cent glasses of beer. Whisky was of course what paid the bills, though it had to be dispensed from bottles kept beneath the bar, in brown paper bags. Even so, a wave of morality would sometimes overtake the authorities, particularly in an election year, and they would raid the beer-joints, confiscating and arresting as they went. The Wheeling police would sometimes be accompanied by county deputies or, if it was necessary to keep the county deputies honest in turn, by state troopers. Every bar in the city got raided a few times except the Hat, because Nick was religious about never missing a payment to Big Bill Lias's agents. Sometimes these field representatives would also force him to accept slot machines (vastly more illegal than whisky). Despite his calm almost somnambulant exterior, Nick always seemed to be looking out the window anxiously, as though expecting rival hoods to appear with sledge-hammers. I didn't make the connection at the time, but now, in my presbyopia, I see that this was another fact he had in common with Father. They were both cool on the surface but nervous underneath, like Bing Crosby.

Nor did I realize then what seems blatant to me now as I look back: that the clientele were so obviously the Second World War generation, with the scars to prove it, literally as well as emotionally and economically. One man, who lived in a walk-up apartment directly across the street, always wore long-sleeve shirts with the sleeves rolled down and buttoned, even on the hottest days; his wife once confessed to my mother that after many years of marriage she'd never seen her husband's bare left arm and was told she wouldn't wish to. Another patron was missing a hand. A third, a burly fellow with tight curls of tough blond hair, had been a mercenary pilot in China, one of General Claire Chennault's Flying Tigers, or so he said. I recall them now as sadly disjointed creatures, able to communicate only by grunt or drunken periphrasis.

Two of the regulars, much older than the others, stand out in my memory. The first was a man about seventy, a former boxer, who would sometimes jog by and say, in answer to my father's polite enquiry, "I'm trainin' for the big one, George, trainin' for the big one," as indeed he seemed to believe. The other was Old Louie. He was about the same age and wore baggy blue pin-stripe trousers supported by a pair of braces that stretched up over his massive belly like two mountain highways. He would arrive at the Hat shortly after the first of the month, once he'd cashed his pension cheque. He would drink for maybe three days, until the money ran out and he was senseless. Then, according to ritual, Nick would call a Burns & Church taxi at his own expense and ask several of the other drunks to help Louie into it so he could be returned to his room. Invariably Louie resisted and would have to be trundled into the car against his wishes. As he was being carried off, he would hurl drunken curses at the rest of the patrons. Louie was an urbanite, like Mother, and the worst name he would think to call anyone was farmer. Jammed into the back seat he'd yell, "You farmers you, you agriculturalists!" As the car pulled away, you could hear him screaming, "*Goddam fucking tillers of the soil!*"

I regret to report that many of the ugly scenes at the Top Hat were Mother's doing, and Nick, with the greatest reluctance at losing such loyal customers, would ask Father to keep her the hell away from there, whereupon some other watering hole would be found for a while. There was Manual's, a bit farther down 29th Street, where men from the Schroeder Casket Works came to drink after loading coffins at the rail siding all day. The alternative was more likely to be Katie's, a place on the other side of the street that offered hookers upstairs as well as booze and steaks below, though I'm not certain that Mother ever twigged to the prostitutes. She was not worldly in sexual matters and sometimes used *nudist* as a substitute for the word *reprobate*, which she did not know. A fellow with his belly up to the bar might indeed be surprised to find this fat drunken women suddenly accosting him and accusing him of being a sun-worshipper. She also believed that male homosexuals were all members of a club, literally; at least once I heard her accuse Father of belonging to it: a response to some new sign, I forget what, that the English part of his personality had flashed its presence. In any case, women with red vinyl boots and lots of cheap perfume would have just struck Mother as being classy. She'd hate them for it, mind you, but she'd think they were classy.

One of these periods of exile from the Top Hat lasted a year. I hate to think what she'd done. The punishment, however, seemed to have no effect on her performance.

CHAPTER TWO

NEWSBOY ALLEY

THE PROGRESSIVE MOVEMENT in American politics was torn apart in 1949 with the defeat of Henry Wallace; in January 1950, Alger Hiss was convicted of perjury and President Harry Truman announced the development of a new weapon a thousand times deadlier than those used on Hiroshima and Nagasaki—the H-bomb. The following month, Klaus Fuchs was arrested for espionage, for supposedly passing secrets to the Soviets. And a few days after that (when I was still only one year old) Senator Joe McCarthy, then a rather obscure Wisconsin politician, addressed a local Republican group in the Colonnade Room of the McLure House in Wheeling. There he announced, to the surprise of many people, including himself perhaps, that he had the names of 205 communists in the State Department. A reporter, Frank Desmond of the Wheeling *Intelligencer*, who was covering the rubber chicken beat at the time, grew suddenly sober. He gave the paper the biggest scoop in its history and was showered with glory (which he bequeathed to his widow, with whom I was slightly acquainted in later times). By 1951, American communists were going underground—those not bound for prison.

In seeking to explain the *locus* in which McCarthyism was born, one historian has unearthed a news item from the previous year telling of an uproar over a chewing gum wrapper. It seems that a citizen had purchased a brand of gum whose packaging showed the flags of the world and listed the various capitals. This particular piece featured the Soviet flag and the hated name Moscow. A minor scandal erupted because this was held to be a trick for propagating godless communism among impressionable Wheelingites. Such was the political atmosphere in which I was growing up.

It seems inconceivable to me that there can ever have been, at any point in the festival of credulity that is America, a more patriotic community than Wheeling. It was also, for instance, the birthplace of the American Legion, the front of whose building—Post No. 1—was in my time decorated with the sentiment NO DRAFT DODGERS HERE—100% AMERICAN VETERANS. I felt out of place from an early age, though how early I find it impossible to say; enlightenment was a process, not a series of revelations.

Beginning when I was about twelve, I railed, silently, against having to begin school each day by reciting the Pledge of Allegiance to the Flag, with right hand over heart, if you can imagine such shameless vexillolatry. When I got caught standing there stubbornly not moving my lips, I would substitute my own subversive version of the text, letting the words get lost in the general chanting. Somewhat later I arranged for one of the teachers to be sent a card announcing that he had been given a gift subscription to a John Birch Society periodical. This was my oblique way of commenting on the political content of his English classes. I was suspended. My political impulses included a certain tendency towards social suicide, as though I had nothing to lose. My speech already set me apart, and when it didn't I was sure to isolate myself through glibness. Class differences always made me feel like an alien. School was skewed towards kids from Out the Pike, local parlance for the modern upper-middle-class areas that hugged National Road, the old turnpike of 1818. I was left to cultivate the company of the few other outcasts. At one school, my companion was a fellow who was fated for a sad end. After graduation, it seemed, he took to killing young girls, and so, like the narrator in the Merle Haggard ballad, turned twenty-one in prison doing life without parole.

Once when I was perhaps ten I received a taste of my father's anger, a rare commodity, after I somehow ruined a tool that he had borrowed from his employers. It was a labelling device that embossed letters and numerals on a continuously fed strip of tin. It was designed for making serial-number plates for large pieces of machinery, but I had been using it to identify all the trees by their Latin names. I was a bookish sort of loner, as much at odds with school as school was with me, and I wandered off on my own, plundering libraries and following an unpredictable course, with one book passionately suggesting some other which would lead urgently to a third. Mother feared and detested such activity as much as I craved it. She actually told me once, in one of her extreme moments, that she was strongly opposed to my learning how to read and write. Oh, the obituary column of the Wheeling

News-Register (her own favourite matter) might be all right, or perhaps the headlines on the trashy tabloids. But stupid as she was, she was wise enough to know that even such reading as that, if left unchecked, might lead—well, to books. I set down these words now scarcely able to warrant that idiocy on the scale I'm describing was possible, but it was.

The search for books pushed me to seek out people who might at least have read ones I couldn't find. To this extent, I sometimes left my shell. In this way I located individuals with some taste for learning which they had been forced to paint over if they were to find even a modest place in the oppressive ignorance of darkest America. Once I learned their secret, they were uniformly kind, my youth and dysfluency notwith-standing.

I got to know one of my father's brother machinists who was using the trade to support himself as a kind of independent anthropologist. Through him I met a court stenographer who led a shadow life as an archae-ologist and whose field-work had produced an enor-mous number of scholarly papers. In the back streets of South Wheeling, where it always seemed to be Novem-ber, there were still a few reminders of a previous epoch, men who wore their hair almost to their shoulders, as they once had done in Serbia or Poland, and aged anarcho-syndicalists and other survivors of the old radi-cal culture that had been destroyed by the Palmer Raids in a great orgy of Americanism after the First World War. One of my best discoveries had once been a reader in one of the stogie factories. Stogies were still made by traditional methods, with the workers sitting at long tables in big airless rooms and paid at piece-rates according to the number of cigars they could roll by the close of each day. In earlier times, such jobs were held by educated people whose foreign birth kept them from more meaningful employment, and it was their custom to select one member of the group to read aloud, with everyone else contributing so many cigars to his or her upkeep. They preferred to hear the classics and general European literature. They had a special affection for Goethe and Schiller of course, but also Stendhal, and from time to time might essay something topical, such as *Die Lage der arbeitenden Klasse in England*. The person I had the most difficulty getting to know was the patriarch of local pawnbrokers. Since arriving in 1908 he had secretly devoted himself to literature, philosophy, music and painting when not hunched over on a high stool, looking at life through a jeweller's loop. His response to decades of anti-Semitism was to emit secretions that formed one hard shell atop another; I was never able to get past the outermost layer but was rewarded for the effort.

The teenager whose crude stirrings I am trying to describe naturally wanted to be a poet, indeed thought he was one already, and even managed to get a few poems published in the type of semi-professional literary magazine often associated with out-of-the-way colleges and universities. For the first and only time in my life, a stranger telephoned to say that she had enjoyed a poem of mine, and in that way I met Mary Tominack, who had the greatest beneficial influence on me of anyone. She was a large lumpy woman who wore the sort of cheap cotton dresses commonly seen in photographs of the Depression. One of the potent events that had informed her life took place in the early 1920s when she was a young girl. The Ku Klux Klan burned a cross in front of her parents' home because they were Poles and Catholics in an anglo and Protestant neighbourhood. Her response was not to cower or even become bitterly defiant but to look for the enzyme that would release humanity into the system. The search brought her heartache as well as gratification. After she was identified as a communist in testimony before the House Un-American Activities Committee, she was literally spit on in the street by such people as didn't avoid her altogether. The *Intelligencer*, by tradition a fearless upholder of the rights of the powerful, had made her existence particularly hard through smears and surveillance. She pushed on.

By the time I met her, she was about fifty and had already exhausted several husbands and still seemed always to have a houseful of children of assorted ages and races. Her entire home, a rotting ramshackle structure on the Island, with the high-water marks of successive floods visible on the side like the growth-rings in a tree, was one enormous office. You wouldn't know it to look at the mess of paper on every flat surface, but her organizational skills were virtually Napoleonic. She was a presence or a force in groups as far apart in their approach as the Congress of Racial Equality and the Sexual Freedom League; the friend, comforter and prodder of agitators, martyrs, refugees, renegades, subversives, outlaws, cranks, dietary reformers and, of course, folk-singers.

How she could afford to do so I can't imagine, but she subscribed to a perplexing array of publications

from the most mainstream to the most deliciously
obscure and not only devoured them in whatever language they appeared but also clipped them for a house-
wide filing system which she alone understood but
which turned out to be remarkably efficient. She would
interrupt the writing of some newsletter, or the comple-
tion of a complicated verbal argument, to run her heavy
frame up or down flights of stairs, emerging moments
later with the incontestable proof that Lyndon Johnson,
Richard Nixon and the coffee interests had conspired to
kill Kennedy right from the beginning. The information was precisely where it should have been, in the old
Quaker Oats carton under the kitchen table on the
screened-in summer porch, next to the box where the
cats peed. She naturally didn't own any cats but looked
after a dozen or so. When the cats' rightful masters and
mistresses came to retrieve them, she converted their
children to vegetarianism and gave them free piano
lessons. She was wonderful.

Her life in the swirl of the present was as vital as her
links to the past were strong. In recent years she had
marched with Martin Luther King in both Selma and
Washington and had often been arrested. But her memories extended back to many figures of the 1930s, including Irving Granich, who as "Mike Gold" became famous
for editing the *Liberator,* and Woody Guthrie. Any survivor of that crowd who was going cross country was
likely to stop by, while a younger generation used her
address as a halfway house and perhaps even as a stop on
the underground railroad, as need dictated. She was part
of the connective tissue between Old Left and New but
also between politics and the arts, by temperament as

well as through her wide range of acquaintances. She was a friend, for example, of two generations of the Dunson family in New York: the father, who ran International Publishers, the literary arm of the Communist Party, and the son, Josh, the editor of *Broadside*, the magazine of protest songs whose regular contributing editors included Bob Dylan.

Vietnam was becoming everyone's obsession. The dictator Diem, whom Lyndon Johnson had once called the Winston Churchill of his people, had been overthrown the same way he had been installed originally, with the connivance of Washington, and the build-up of U.S. troops went ticking along as Buddhist monks set fire to themselves in protest. One's tendency was to oppose the war because the government waged it and one's elders condoned it. Under Mary's tutelage I got involved more deeply and learned shame for the killing and destruction that was going on and at times purblind anger over our powerlessness as individuals to do anything at all about it. She naturally knew a couple of brave Christian radicals connected with the local Jesuit college, though they feared censure by their order and rebuke by the Bishop of Wheeling. In a characteristic gesture, for her natural inclination was always towards coalition, she brought them together with everyone else she could convince to take part, and put her cell together with others in places like Pittsburgh and Cleveland as part of what was in those early days a more narrow and more religiously focused movement than it would be even a short time later. I was thus the most junior person in the smallest link in what was still a very fragile chain, but I felt I was growing for once.

I was befriended by one of the Catholic professors in the group, John McIntyre, who possessed the touching faith in human nature that only natural anarchists ever seem to achieve. Through him I moved into an overlapping circle of people associated with the two other small campuses in the area, and in that way met the preposterous figure of Arthur Tarlow. What a pattern of images that old scoundrel's name evokes. Tarlow was a tramp history teacher who on falling into disgrace at some college would land with a thud at an even less distinguished one. By that means, he had worked his way from someplace in the South, whence he originated, through New England and then across the Midwest and back. He wore spectacles in small square frames of thin wire which contributed to the general impression that he might once have been a leprechaun until expelled from the band on grounds of moral turpitude. He sounded a bit like Tennessee Williams, with vowels that went on forever. When he spoke he would roll his ovoid eyes upward as though in disbelief at his own last utterance, which was in fact likely to be one that an earthbound person would find hard to credit. He also shared Williams's sexual orientation and had an ornate and ironic homosexual wit. I don't know how old he was, but he had served in the Second World War. "The Nazis," he said to me once, "had no sense of whimsy."

Tarlow lived at the only place such a person could, the Windsor Hotel, which had seen better days even longer ago than any of its residents, including Tarlow, were able to remember. Its entrance was now on Main though it was built to face Water Street, with a high-columned verandah giving off onto the river. But the steamboats that once tied up at the Wharf, or levee, were generations gone. All you could see through the ragged curtains in Tarlow's apartment was the occasional tug, pushing a load of coal barges upriver through the fog and hooting mournfully as it passed beneath the bridges.

He specifically forbade the hotel maid from ever entering his apartment—I believe he once threatened her with the cord of his well-worn dressing gown, using it as a whip—and so the place was thoroughly disordered, with stacks of books used as tables and the ungraded papers of his students jammed into the cupboards above the hot-plate. One of his principal recreations was trying to put the nash on Bill Forbes, another character who soon became one of my friends. Bill was a young painter, Black, who sometimes worked in construction when necessary, and when truly desperate would extort money from people in bars by impersonating a minister of the Gospel. He had a clerical collar and credentials from some non-existent holy-roller church and gave pretty convincing hell-fire sermons. He would then pass the collection plate. If feeling especially bold, he might also sell the Gideon Bibles he had stolen from various Holiday Inns. He was thoroughly heterosexual, but that didn't seem to keep Tarlow from trying, much to his sorrow. When rebuked yet again, Tarlow would scour the bars in the red-light district in Centre Wheeling, usually with only enough luck to get picked up by the cops. His response to getting busted was always to make sexual advances to the arresting officer or officers, a tactic that seldom did him much good except in that he seemed to enjoy being bloodied. Bill really liked him, as one had to do, and cared about him. And so it went.

The police—we called them the brownshirts, after Hitler's henchmen—were on to Tarlow, were at least more than a little suspicious of Bill, and were aware of me, too, since they routinely staked out Mary's house on the Island. It's difficult to say who led them to whom, but suddenly the heat was on. I got rousted one morning in a laundromat Out the Pike where I suppose I looked as though I didn't belong (I didn't). Bill, being Black, was handled more roughly and sometimes got taken to the station. He would come back with fanciful tales of his incarceration. "I get to the cop-shop, man, and all the brownshirts are watching reruns of *I Love Lucy* on a confiscated TV. One of them is on the floor lying on his stomach with a colouring book. 'Hey Sarge, you got my blue crayola?' and the desk sergeant answers, 'Blow man, I ain't seen it' and the one on the floor says, 'Whaddya you mean you ain't seen it? How-daya 'spect me to finish my pitcher?' and the Sarge says, 'Hey, so don't draw no skies.' It gave me a warm inner glow to see our tax dollars thus employed."

Bill was forever on the prowl for sex and excitement and I was sometimes able to prevail on him to take me along. There were, however, certain inherent obstacles in such ventures. One was the fact that there were only one or two so-called zebra bars, where Blacks were per-mitted by reluctant custom to drink with whites. Another was the fact that I was still only about fifteen or sixteen, and looked it, being gangly and with an enor-mous Adam's apple. Thus we could drink only in places of low resort whose owners weren't interested in observing the legal niceties. For practical purposes this meant a joint on the Island grandiloquently named the Yacht Club. It was in fact a small cement block building with a bar and a rickety walkway over the water leading down to a converted coal barge, and was run by a former acrobat named Walker Dick whose forebears had worked on the river, as steamboat captains and such, for generations. He had been married many times and had once owned a small circus. It was difficult to say which of these vitae the absurd local establishment found more odious. The mere fact that he was ostracized was enough to endear him to us.

Wheeling is one of the few hilly cities in the world where the poor live atop the hills, overlooking the well-off down below. As the east-west streets ran back from the river, they crawled up the steep face of a mountain to a rank slum near the summit. Much to our disgust, the older generation often called this area Niggertown. In those days there was only a single housing project there, of recent origin but already in chaos and decay; otherwise the maze of original frame buildings stood pretty much undisturbed by changes in municipal fashion, with porches rotting away, ceilings sagging, the very houses themselves slanting dangerously as they clung to the precipitous and broken streets. It was an article of faith that the fire department would take its time responding to calls from the area in the hope that the whole place would be burned out. Bill had grown up there, on Charles Street, near what had been the legally segregated Black high school, which was now integrated in name but not in fact. His birthright gave him free access to some curious places around town where I was allowed when I was with him, although he couldn't enter the equivalent white establishments even as a guest.

There was the Beau Brummel Social Club, with its ridiculous suggestion of grandiosity. But the name as well as the music were in the same tradition as the Benjamin Harrison Social Club, the Pittsburgh after-hours joint where Maxine Sullivan (who introduced "Jeepers Creepers" with Louis Armstrong) got her start. And there was a place that sold crawfish out of a bucket down in South Wheeling by the river, where the hobo jungles used to be, the territory described so memorably in some of Davis Grubb's fiction and a couple of James Wright's poems. One night a bunch of us went from there to a hookers' hotel near the old Centre Market. Its only badge of identity was an orange neon sign spelling out HOTEL; it had no other name and so Tarlow began referring to it as the Hotel Hotel and then Le Grand Hotel Hotel, making long-winded and drunken comparisons between it and the Excelsior in Rome. Despite outings with Bill, I never quite succeeded in losing my virginity, such as it was, until both of us became infatuated with a go-go dancer in a bar downtown, the sort of dive that reinvented itself on Fridays, when the busloads of tourists and foreigners came to town for the WWVA Jamboree and the owner put out signs reading NO COVER NO MINIMUM CANADIAN $$$ ACCEPTED AT PAR. I can see this dancer yet. It seemed to us that she was beautiful, though she chewed gum, even while standing in a cage suspended from the ceiling, swinging her arms up over her head, first one and then the other, in approximate time to the music.

To no one else's surprise, but at some cost to my natural romanticism, she turned out to be a hooker on the side. She said she had never done it with a Black guy and Bill very kindly got me included in the one low price as a sort of supercargo, though I still fancied that what she had in mind was a *boff de politesse*. We used Tarlow's apartment, with me first waiting in the corridor, looking stupid, until the two of them had finished. Tarlow, returning at the appointed hour, referred to our activity as "fucking in the biblical sense."

All this while Bill was painting frantically. I never again saw anything like his work until I learned about Beryl Cook's in England years later. He affected membership in the folk tradition and the naiveté was quite believable; one had to be hip to see the hipness from which he drew. He gave me several of his canvases, which I lost one by one in various moves and periods of turmoil over the years, but the example I remember most vividly was one he wouldn't part with. He called it the *Adoration of the Bookies*. It was a Nativity scene that included the faces of various Market Street characters, members of the gaming community. I thought he was a genius and he repaid the compliment in kind. We were young.

Eventually I got out of school, putting an end to the double life I was leading, and tried desperately to find a job. I made lists of twenty businesses each day to call on. The closest I came to employment was when a tree trimmer, under contract to the electric utility, gave me a couple days' work as a high-climbing apprentice. After a week or so I was mightily discouraged. My father suggested I try a friend of his whom he had prevailed on once or twice when he was out on strike. The business was on Water Street, near the Wharf, where it had begun in the early steamboat days selling rope and such to the captains, and it still did a bit of ship chandlery in addition to a wholesale appliance business. But Father's contact had died. With a guitar player I met at Mary's, I launched a plan to make money selling country songs to one of the fly-by-night music publishers commonly found in half-empty office buildings. Our best collaboration was called "I See by Your Leg Irons You're a Prisoner" but though the publisher held out the promise of fifty dollars for the copyright we were never able to collect. Of another of our joint efforts, I recall only one line: "She made a virtue of necessity / and a fool outta me." I spent some time in Pittsburgh looking for groups of writers to be part of, but had little success. Sam Hazo, the Catholic poet and anthologist, dominated the established circle and had no reason to take me seriously, while the underground was led by Ron Caplan, a figure of the day whom I never quite caught up with and who had close links to places like the Coach House Press in Toronto, which had recently opened. I went to Cleveland, too, where Jim Lowell's Asphodel Bookshop in the Arcade was the centre of activity and the leading personality was d.a. levy, who was busted for obscenity at about that time and later shot himself. I hitched to Toronto as well, for Mary had been feeding me clippings and pamphlets about the Vietnam exiles there, and I made some contacts. But I came back to Wheeling, hating the place more than ever. For a while I was ready to take Bill's advice and beg work as a non-union construction labourer, making a good wage for a few days' backbreaking toil here and there. I was resigned to this when I was given the opportunity to pursue a lucrative career in the fast-growing field of commercial dish-washing.

Somebody tipped me off that they needed a dish-washer at Louie's diner, where Short Market Street met Stone's Alley, and the intelligence proved accurate. I would start in the afternoon and work until they closed at night and get twenty dollars a week. The original Louie had been gone for years, but the present owner had inherited his name along with the business. In addition to this Louie, who was the counterman and soda jerk, the only other staff besides myself was the cook. He was a large fellow with a shaven head and a swastika tattooed on the lobe of one ear. Before starting the shift each day, he would give his massive arms and torso a thick coat of glistening oil. Then he would repair to the alley out back and take an almost sexual delight in sharpening all the knives and cleavers on a whetstone. When he failed to show up about my fifth or sixth day, I became the cook as well as the dishwasher. The promotion carried no increase in pay, but then the cooking might consist only of scraping mould off the meat loaf, adding an ice cream scoop of reheated mashed potatoes and covering it all with gelatinous gravy. During the slack periods midway between lunch and dinner and again between dinner and closing, I would read or write for a few moments if I had caught up on my washing. I hadn't been working there more than two weeks when Louie came into the back unexpectedly and caught me writing a poem, an activity that to him seemed as shameful as masturbation on the job. I was fired.

As would happen so often later in life whenever I was fired or fiercely attacked, my emergency generators kicked in and I made instant decisions aimed at defending myself: a legacy, I believe, from having grown up under the constant threat of Mother's explosive temper. In this case I went immediately, almost without thinking, to the Centre Market square where John Palsa, a local hoodlum and former professional fighter who lived in Bethlehem not far from us, had a storefront full of old golf-bags, rusty mufflers and unidentified bits of secondhand plumbing—a not very convincing cover for whatever business he was running out of the back. I knew that he was also engaged in some sort of restaurant. Small-time hoods often ran greasy spoons, for they always needed a legitimate place of business through which to filter cash. I found him wearing a silk shirt and alligator shoes, sitting in his store full of rubbish. He recognized me, thought I was a good kid, and told me that he'd put me to work as a dishwasher at the Academy on Market Street. This was a much grander resolution than I could have wished for, not merely because now I would get twenty-five dollars a week as well as meals, but because the Academy was an important place on the underworld map, the headquarters of Paul Hankish.

"Big Bill Lias was more famous than the president of the United States—whoever that was at the time." That remarkable sentence was uttered by one of Mother's younger sisters, reminiscing about her girlhood in the early 1940s. She could also remember seeing Alma Henderson, Wheeling's grandest and most notorious madam, taking her charges shopping in a red limousine. Alma, who used to send glamorous nude photos of herself to her more important clients, the ones who sat in high leather chairs in the Fort Henry Club clipping their bond coupons, was long gone from the scene when I became aware of such things. Indeed it was vivid evidence of her decline, and the passing of the old order generally, when her son, in the course of robbing a supermarket, shot and killed an acquaintance of my parents. As for Big Bill, he was still around, still had money despite the government seizure of his assets, still had powerful connections. But he was a diminishing force. Speculation about matters like these, and about who had replaced him, and who controlled whoever replaced him, was everyday conversation at the dinner table and the beer-joint.

What seemed clear is that though Lias ran West Virginia and enjoyed a marsupial relationship with one of the state's two U.S. senators, he was himself sometimes indebted to Pennsylvania, at least indirectly, for one of that state's own senators spent his time away from Washington in a suite at the William Penn Hotel in Pittsburgh, giving orders to gangsters through a bank of telephones. The various tax-evasion and deportation proceedings against him made Lias a national figure ("I ain't been no angel," he informed *Life* magazine). That in turn made him still more vulnerable. And then, too, he was growing old and ill. He had always adamantly refused to allow drugs in the city, a restriction his younger rivals thought absurd. "The day I knew Big Bill was finished," a friend of mine said, "was when I walked into the men's room of the Pythian Building and there was a fourteen-year-old kid shooting heroin, trying to look nonchalant." Big Bill's heir apparent or heir presumptive, it wasn't clear which, was the aforesaid Paul Hankish.

Lias had once run his empire from Zellers, a Market Street restaurant and casino where patrons could proceed from one level of illegality to another simply by continuing to climb the stairs. The place was so named because it had once belonged to Dutch Zellers, who had started out as a pickpocket on riverboats in the 1890s but who eventually, following a well-publicized conversion by Billy Sunday, became first a policeman and then an evangelist in his own right. Now, the bar at street level was operated by Hankish. But in the casino above—where in my extreme youth I would visualize tuxedoed millionaires and their seeing-eye mistresses, sipping mock turtle soup and listening to jazz—the windows were boarded up and the leather banquettes mouldering. Still, as far as could be determined, this was a structure in which no legal activity had taken place for forty years or so. That seemed a remarkable record for a building in the private sector, until one considered a certain whorehouse in Centre Wheeling that had been in business uninterruptedly since the red-light district moved there from the Upper Market in about 1905.

The passing of the torch from Lias to Hankish was not entirely smooth, however, for several other organizations had tried to muscle in on the big fellow's set-up. In my childhood these lesser groups were forever smashing one another's pinball machines or blowing the fronts out of one another's warehouses, until finally there was only one serious contender, the Ohio gang, based in Bridgeport, one of the tough little towns on the opposite bank of the river. Tempers flared.

One morning in 1964 (I rely on newspaper clippings for the date), Hankish made the classic mistake of starting his automobile himself. An explosion took off the whole front end of the car and both of his legs above the knee. A person or persons unknown, whom every bookmaker up and down Market Street could name, had wired dynamite to the ignition.

The Academy, where John Palsa, a Hankish lieutenant, kindly put me to work, was across the street from the old Zellers and was Hankish's official address. Hankish was often written about in the papers—"prominent sportsman" was the preferred style for rackets figures, or sometimes "prominent Wheeling gambler"—but he wasn't a public personage the way Lias had been in his prime, not someone adolescents pestered for his autograph, and so I had never actually seen him until I reported for work. At about midnight, the people at the bar suddenly grew quiet. The boys in the backroom laid down the dice and the pool-shooters brought their cues to parade rest. There was Hankish, dark, balding, surprisingly young, walking towards his private office to go over the night's receipts. He strode on artificial legs using aluminum crutches, the sort with hand-grips halfway up, at right angles to the shafts. The Academy had a hard tile floor composed of tiny white octagons. One of his crutches had lost its protective rubber tip, so that when Paul moved he made a metallic *ping-ping* noise. The regulars could hear him coming at a considerable distance, like Marley's Ghost or the crocodile in *Peter Pan*.

The Academy was divided in two, with the bar featuring large expensive mirrors, a billiard room and the Back Room on one side, the restaurant on the other. It was typical of such places that the restaurant was oversupplied with expensive kitchen equipment that was kept in new condition because it was so seldom used, even though there were three cooks and the one on the 11 p.m. to 7 a.m. shift would frequently be called on to make big meals on no notice at some improbable hour.

There was already a dishwasher in place when I arrived but, as Mister Palsa explained, he was a spastic and the task was too much for him. Still, he went on, he wouldn't feel right firing the poor fellow as he had known the boy's father (had probably shot him, I thought). But I could have the job six days a week and the spastic would be the relief man on Mondays. Since the nature of the business and the weight of precedent made the proprietors careful about income tax complications, I would be paid by cheque.

First I would sweep out the place and then haul meat from the walk-in freezer in the basement and take the garbage out to the alley. I was kept busy, though the actual dishwashing was not onerous because so few people came there to eat—that would be like going to the candy store–bookie joint to buy a box of sweets. Tuesdays, following my day off, could be trying, however, since I had to redo the dishes done by the spastic the previous night. He would replace them in the cabinet with pieces of pie and soapsuds still stuck to them, so that a tall stack of saucers could be picked up like a concertina.

I would also cater to the boys in the Back Room, fighting through the cigar smoke to bring them sandwiches and drinks from the bar. Sometimes I would also help out as rack boy in the poolroom or as boardman, writing the odds at the various races on a big slate while standing on a wheeled stepladder from which hung a bucket of water for soaking chalk. The other part of my daily routine was scrubbing the toilets.

I've never known a place where nicknames, which often served as aliases, were more numerous or had such interesting etymologies. There was a fellow called Mouse whose real name was Mauser and another called J.R. simply because he was Somebody Jr., and the people with whom he associated weren't literate enough to know what the abbreviation meant. There was a man called Shooter not because he liked his shooter of whisky nor because he was a gunman (though he may have been, coincidentally). Rather, he was highly excitable and would always enter a crap game yelling, "New shooter! New shooter up!" A patron named Spanish, who looked like a forty-five-year-old version of the comic strip character Henry, was also known as Dos, a misconstruction of Doze or possibly of Dose, as in Overdose, which is perhaps what he had once tried to do. With regard to a person known as Gutter Smith, my researches failed me; I prefer to think the name betrayed his origins and wasn't a corruption of Got Her, but I fear the worst.

The most vivid in my memory is Walleye (after the fish to which he bore a resemblance) but then he loomed the largest at the time. He spoke in the manner of a 1950s jazzman. In summer he wore glossy black shoes with black socks, plaid bermuda shorts and, as in the other seasons, a knit shirt with a little porpoise embroidered on the left breast. The costume was always topped off by a Tyrolean skiing hat complete with a tiny feather. He had begun life as a runner for Bill Lias and was now a small-time fence and freelance bookie, one of a number who used the pay phones at the Academy in exchange for a percentage of the take. He seemed to be in almost telepathic communication with places like Arlington Park and Hialeah, and it was said by way of an advertising claim that he could give you odds that the sun wouldn't rise. It was only by receiving stolen goods that he ever got into legal difficulties and then only when he tried to enter the big time. He had always been the sort of fellow who had access to packs of cigarettes—without tax seals—at twenty cents each, part of some hijacked shipment. Once came a rumour of a room full of air conditioners; another time, a duffle bag of Swiss watch movements. Twenty years after all of this, some newspaper clippings reached me about his recent activity. A large team of heavily armed brownshirts stove in the door of his dismal furnished room and found him lying abed with a fortune in artworks missing since a recent series of burglaries.

One of the cops said in disbelief, considering the surroundings, "Where'd you *get* all this stuff?"

Walleye replied, "Hey, I'm a collector. It's a hedge against inflation."

One day I returned home just before dusk and could hear Mother's nightly temper spilling out into the road, some distance away. When I went inside, however, I learned that I'd been mistaken. It was her laughter, not her arguing, that had reached me through the walls, the sound distorted as it lost its shape in the open air. A trivial incident but one I've remembered because it fell so unexpectedly. It was, after all, six o'clock, when the fighting always began. I was in the habit of steeling myself for the tension that filled the place, tension that ranged from the silent anger of clenched muscles to the violence of protruding eyes and set jaws. Such temporary relief that day was a gift and also a fluke. And so it was, I believe, that the stress finally caught up with Father, aided by cigarettes and alcohol to the extent these represented separate hazards. He had a heart attack. He was forty-nine and was saved only by the quick action of his friend Alec, who scooped him up from the parking lot of the plant and ran with him in his arms to the nursing station. I saw him early that evening in his hospital room. Whether from medication or from fear, a bit of both I suppose, he was in a state that fell between delirium and hysteria. He thought he was dying, and looking at me kept saying "Poor Doug, Poor Doug" in a way that's always touched me with its selflessness but left me to puzzle over his exact meaning.

He was kept in hospital for weeks before being sent home with instructions to avoid stairs, but Mother objected to him sleeping on the sofa on the ground floor and so that arrangement lasted only a short time. Periodically he would see the doctor, who would advise him to get more rest, to which he would reply with a joke. His tinny world of humour became tinnier over the next year, his attempts at jokes cornier and cornier.

He would forget himself and repeat the same ones again and again; his listeners would pretend to smile and he would pretend to laugh. He had lost his excess weight but the change made him look even sicker, his clothes now hung so loosely. He started back at the plant but his co-workers made an agreement among themselves to take all the strenuous jobs. There was no fundamental change at home, however, only the same pattern of ominous lulls and violent abuse. There was only this new twist: that if the argument lasted to 2:00 or 3:00 a.m., he would take a blanket and pad downstairs, though the noise might follow him down for another hour, to just a couple of hours before he had to begin the working day. On still other nights, however, he would wander about in the small hours even though Mother lay sleeping. Restless and sick from something that wasn't revealed in the diagnosis, he would find himself unable to lie down or sit still, and would finally sleep standing up, leaning against the fridge door with his head on his arm.

Just as he kept up working at his job, for he couldn't afford to quit, so too he continued, even increased, his work with the union, an organization that earned Mother's ridicule and jealousy. One day he announced that he would be going out to an important meeting the following night, a strike vote if my memory is correct. Such an absence was rare and he was careful to say that, barring the unexpected, he would return by a certain hour, perhaps ten o'clock. Over the course of the evening, I watched with mounting anxiety as Mother moved with quick little steps from object to object, first straightening things, then unstraightening them and lastly banging them this way and that, a sign that her plunging blood sugar and rising bile had crossed somewhere in the blackness. As ten o'clock neared, she went from room to room and reset whatever timepieces the house had—the ship's clock that had belonged to Grandfather Fetherling, the plastic one on the wall near the kitchen sink, a couple of others embedded in radios, the clock in their bedroom. I was horrified and fascinated to observe her mind at work. The plan, clearly, was to create the illusion that it was later than it actually was, thereby justifying an even louder argument than the normal one that his absence had deprived her of. Except that in her bibulous state she had set all these clocks to different times. When Father returned at ten, the abuse struck him like a blast of oppressive heat as soon as he entered. In a moment, looking at first one clock and then another, he realized what she'd done. It was the only time I ever saw him cry.

Another night, Mother stormed out of the house, pausing only to slam the door more than once; she said that as she was being held prisoner on this damn hilltop she would walk all the way into the city, and started off in the direction of Suicide Hill. Father felt he had no choice but to follow. Fortunately, he reached her before she got to the point beyond which even a healthy person would have huffed and puffed climbing back up again.

One day he had a doctor's appointment immediately after work, and as I was in the city to begin my shift at the Academy, he and I had dinner together alone, for the first time in our lives. We sat in a fast food place near the hospital, overlooking what skyline there

was and the river just beyond. He talked about characters he'd known, such as a salesman who always introduced himself as "a traveller in risqué novelties," which
indeed he was, or a fellow whose avocation was trying
to convince others that the birth of Christ had taken
place at a specific moment of a particular day in what
would be our July, a claim for which he was never without incomprehensible evidence, crumpled in his pock-
ets. I tried to bring the conversation around to Mother,
but he was nervous as usual and in a hurry to reminisce.

Finally I asked bluntly why the two of them didn't
separate and get a divorce. I had made the suggestion a
couple of times when I was small, when people were
surprised that I knew the meaning of the words. This
was different. It seemed to me the situation was desperate, though of course I was acting out of concern for my
own welfare as well as his. The two of us could get a
place to live, I said. It would be the two of us since Dale
was overseas now in the navy. I thought I knew of a
small apartment. I said there would be enough money
to support Mother and still live apart if we played our
cards right, not knowing whether the statement was
true. But he wouldn't listen. He said that they'd gone to
a marriage counsellor once but that she'd kept insulting
the man.

"The next time I see the doctor I'll ask him to write
her a prescription for some happy pills."

Amphetamines.

And I believe he did so, but of course that was no
solution, not even temporarily.

———

In addition to hoodlums and ward-heelers and their hangers-on, the Academy also attracted a number of newspapermen, including a splenetic columnist on the *News-Register*, who had drunk his way there from the Philadelphia *Inquirer*. There were rumours later, after his death, that he had been on the payroll of the Ohio gang in their war against Big Bill Lias and his successors. I don't know if the stories were true, but anyone could see that he'd shinnied up the local establishment and had a lot of power which he enjoyed exercising.

One evening he appeared, as advertised, to act as celebrity referee in a high-stakes pool game between Don Willis, the eastern states champ, and Wee Willie Nassif, the local favourite. Nassif was a diminutive man, five-feet-two or -three, so short that the sign NO MASSE SHOTS could not possibly have been hung there for his benefit. His pinstripe trousers came up to the middle of his chest and he always wore his hat indoors.

The room looked like a Hogarth engraving of a cock-fight. Spectators were jammed shoulder to shoulder. Those occupying the high seats held fat bouquets of currency in both fists. Of the others, some stood on chairs dragged in from the restaurant and the remainder took their chances with the smoke, which cut the room into thick layers. Wee Willie won the break and ran nineteen or twenty balls at twenty dollars a ball. Then it was Willis's turn. He was still at it after a half-hour or so.

This was a swank cultural event, as important as any first night, and I did a gold-rush business ferrying drinks from the bar. But however preferable that was to some of my lesser duties (for one thing, it brought me gratuities), it wasn't what I hoped to do in life. I thought of myself as a writer. I was gradually pulling together a thick manuscript of poems that I proposed to entitle *Sturdy Cripples*. The phrase came from Coleridge, who praised Donne as "Rhyme's sturdy cripple, fancy's maze and clue;/ Wit's forge and fire-blast, meaning's press and screw." The term seemed to me to have a more forceful application in terms of the lives of people I was familiar with. But I wanted to try every type of writing, not only poetry, so as to be led naturally to whatever form seemed appropriate for the immediate purpose. I needed some place where I could get training, and I had my eye set on one of the newspapers. I had read enough totally obsolete books to know that this was how one proceeded.

Following the match, I debated whether I should approach the columnist. Fearing rejection, I hesitated. It wasn't long afterwards, however, that I overheard part of a conversation between two customers in the restaurant while I was mopping the floor. There was an old fellow (in his forties!) with a faint grey moustache. He was talking to a young guy, obviously a colleague. He was making a point about the relative advantages of working on an AM rather than a PM. I noticed where they went when they left: across Market Street and down Newsboy Alley.

I saw Jimmy Simon, a runner and very small-time bookie, standing where he'd been standing for years, outside Fette's Newsstand, far enough away to pick up on any activity in the street, close enough to hear the ringing of the pay phones inside. I asked him who the guy with the moustache was and he told me. "Bob Terry." I waited days for him to come back in for a cup of coffee when I was on duty. He treated me kindly and told me I should see Haven Thompson at the *Intelligencer*.

Thompson (it's a pleasure to remember him here) was about forty-five, lean, rugged and powerful, suggesting an eagle that had been up all night. I simply stood at his desk until he noticed me and I could fumble out my request. He had no job to give, of course. But as one who was reading the classics among newspapermen's autobiographies, I knew precisely what to do. Every night, as soon as my duties at the Academy would permit, I sneaked back into the newsroom and hovered in his field of peripheral vision, gently reminding him of my existence, waiting to be pressed into service for any purpose, however humble. I was determined to hang about like a stray dog until the proprietors wearied of throwing me out into the street. Certainly it didn't take long to become a familiar object of derision among the staff, a state that delighted me as it proved I was being noticed. In two weeks, my belief in tradition was justified: the editor concluded that my desperation to be on his newspaper was adequate to such a noble ambition. The sports department was short-handed, and I was given a telephone headset and pressed into service taking down box scores from high school athletic events. No job as such was mentioned, no money discussed. Still, I smiled inwardly, knowing that I had won myself a permanent place, though I very nearly spoiled the opportunity.

The next night I came in as usual and was collared by Cliff McWilliams, the red-haired sports editor, who sent me to cover a football game at the Island Stadium.

This was a different matter from typing players' names as they were fed to me over the phone. The simple truth was that I didn't know how football was played, didn't know the rules, didn't know how many innings or periods constituted a game. I doubt that I could retrieve a better proof of how remote I was from the interests of mainstream America, in fact antagonistic to the culture, so called, and it equally so to me. I sat in the press-box, staring anxiously at the printed form on which I was expected to record the manoeuvres of the various players and other vital information. At half-time (a term I knew) a kindly man from a radio station took pity on me when I explained my dilemma and let me copy his information onto my sheet and look over his shoulder for the second half. I never saw him again and have never remembered his name if indeed I ever heard it, but he has always had my gratitude. I've never known whether Cliff McWilliams suspected what had gone on. I imagine that he did and chose to exercise compassion. The decision was ironic since it was he, before Haven Thompson succeeded him as editor of the paper, who had hounded my friend Mary Tominack with a kind of vigilante intensity. He surely would have been hostile if he'd known of my involvement with her. At that time, however, I had yet to become notorious in Wheeling.

Thompson said he had a good report about me from McWilliams and would take me on as a reporter on the night trick. I felt very proud when he sent me to the business office with a letter instructing them to enter me on the payroll as a reporter at eighty dollars a week. A reporter. It sounded wonderful. The money sounded fine as well, a 40 per cent increase over my earnings from the Academy, though after deductions the figure was $67.75. Looking back from even short retrospect, it would amaze me that I should ever have been a reporter, given that I usually couldn't talk on the telephone, was terrified of strangers and had no special interest in the facts—was actually quite hostile to the old-fashioned tyranny of meaningless information devoid of texture, discrimination or style—but then perhaps I was no more unlikely a guest than the *Intelligencer* was a host.

Like the other Wheeling paper and what seemed a majority of those in the state, it had been owned by H.C. Ogden, a queer combination of robber baron and reformer whose initials did not, as his enemies used to insist, stand for Hard Cash. He had died in the 1940s, but his portrait still scrutinized everyone entering the newsroom. His proxy on Earth was his grandson, the publisher, a youthful thirty-one, whom the editorial-page editor, who started in the business in 1911, called the Old Man, for such was the habit of a lifetime.

The structure on Main Street was of about the same vintage as the editorial page editor; it connected through a series of doors to a separate mechanical plant in back. This in turn gave way to a building on Market Street: the publisher's bank—literally, he was the president of it and kept his office upstairs, over the vault. To sentimental cynics, this complex was known as the Ogden School of Journalism. For various reasons, including the fact that it was the headquarters and flag-ship of the chain, it seemed to attract people on their way up and others on their way down.

Just beyond the reach of my own memory, for instance, was a former diplomat, his foreign service career in yellowed tatters, who insisted on writing his copy in longhand. I do remember another former diplomatist, Malcolm Brice, who had worked on the Montreal *Herald* and the Ottawa *Journal* early in the century and then served in the American embassy in Dublin. Then there was the eccentric business editor who devoted himself to the promotion of what he called the Midland Canal, a scheme that, if ever approved by Washington, would link the Ohio River with the Atlantic and make international ports of Wheeling and Steubenville. Our region editor, it was said, remembered back to the early 1920s when James Thurber was the *Intelligencer*'s stringer for Ohio politics, during the period when he was working his way from the Columbus *Dispatch* to the *New Yorker*. This region editor had been on the paper so long, in fact, that he had memorized all the possible signals emitted by the fire-alarm box that went off in the newsroom whenever an alarm was sounded; when the racket began, he would put down his pencil, chew his harelip, and listen for a moment. "Forty-fifth and Wood," he would finally say. "The Christian Steinmetz Cigar Box Factory." He'd then tell the reporter the number of the nearest pay phone to the scene, should it be necessary to elicit a first-hand account from some passerby.

These humans, it seemed to me, were sacred relics of a profane past and older than the furniture, which was decrepit. They went hand in glove with a lot of bright younger people whom Haven Thompson had attracted to the place in his campaign, somewhat over the publisher's dead body, I believe, of attempting to make the paper a model of what one in its circulation class should be. They had found themselves there after coming from points as far apart as Connecticut and Florida. One fellow had gone to Cornell with Richard Fariña, the folksinger who was Joan Baez's brother-in-law, and was rumoured to be the original of Gnossos Popodoupolis, the crazy sixties anti-hero in Fariña's new novel *Been Down So Long It Looks Like Up to Me* (which means that he must have been there at the same time as Thomas Pynchon too).

I wrote hundreds of obituaries, possibly thousands, learning about such matters as the various ways the requiem mass is celebrated in the Roman, Greek and Armenian traditions, and I became well known in mortuary circles. At one time it had been the custom for every white undertaker to appear just before Christmas and leave a bottle of bourbon on the obit desk (for some reason, the Black undertakers were expected to give gin instead). The way this practice had died out was the only evidence of the new spirit of reform that was always said to be rampant in the city. One would still see undertakers in person, however, when the hour was late and the deadline nigh and it was especially important that a deceased, usually a bigwig, make it into the first edition. In one such emergency situation I met Sandra. Her father had a funeral parlour across the river and was also a small-time radio evangelist. Much to her embarrassment, he sent her over one night with some details about a client, and we fell into easy conversation—always a sign with me of a potential friendship.

She worked part-time as a lifeguard at a hotel swimming pool. As the job occupied her only in the afternoons, she wasn't bound to keep regular hours, and was thus free to join me in many of my nocturnal assignments and pursuits. We spent a lot of time together in hospital emergency rooms. There was seldom any trace of the specific news I was sent to such places to fetch, but at least there was a lesson to be had. The lesson was that a knife wound in any place except the heart, serious though it might look, is usually quite survivable, but that a corresponding gunshot wound, however superficial it might seem at first, is always much worse than it appears, given the massive cell damage caused by even the smallest calibre bullet fired from a great distance.

One of my duties on the lobster shift was to make the last check with the police. Around midnight, earlier on Sundays, I would scoot up Newsboy Alley to the cop-shop and ask to see the green sheets detailing recent complaints, accidents and arrests. There was seldom much activity at that hour, and I would often go through the motions of exchanging light banter with Icehouse Hixenbaugh, a portly old desk sergeant, so called because his family had once operated an ice business in South Wheeling. He suffered from a strange condition that I assumed, in my callowness, was proof of stupidity, but now understand was probably a developmental disability akin to dyslexia: he spoke and wrote in redundancies. For example, if there was no one to cover the desk when he needed to nip out for a beer, he would tape a crudely lettered sign to the door, BACK IN FIVE MINUTES OF TIME. Not five minutes of pork chops or five minutes of red-dog slag. I remember one weekend asking him with a cheery voice whether anything was going on. "Not much," he said, flipping through the paperwork on his clipboards, "except that the vice boys have knocked over a whorehouse of ill repute." The phrase has remained with me ever since as a perfect metaphor for journalism. No ordinary whorehouse, mind you, but one of ill repute.

Sandra and I would arrange to steal moments together wherever and whenever we could, depending on her movements and my workload. I remember long talks we had on the wooden bench in the detective bureau, down the hall from the counter where Icehouse stood guard. On one occasion we talked about poetry, but I can't recall what it was I was supposed to be doing at the time. We spent at least one memorable evening necking in a car during a stake-out, waiting for the cops to arrive with their sledgehammers and smash the slot machines at a road-house. The tip was bogus. It wasn't an election year and the brownshirts never showed. Just as well.

Another time she came along when I had to cover a large gathering, a fish fry or an ox roast perhaps, of the local Democratic machine. That was a pleasant assignment to draw because the political science practised there was always a delight for anyone with a sense of the picaresque. One of the men who served as governor in my youth was discovered years later driving a taxi in Chicago; another went to prison with fourteen of his officials and friends on charges of fraud and misuse of funds. The mechanism, with all its peculiarities, always survived such changes. Perhaps it even throve on them. I was too young to have seen it at first hand but heard vivid testimony, for it was all around, of the way John Kennedy had purchased the state in his race for the crucial presidential primary in 1960. At a given signal, his father's men had fanned out to every airfield and train station with bags of cash, lots of it. The cash went to the members of the county sheriffs' association, the same officials who sometimes let their prisoners out to help put up campaign posters. The sheriffs in turn would distribute the loot among those most likely to exercise their franchise in the proper fashion. It was like a para-military operation. So indeed was West Virginia politics. Everybody was in the pocket of somebody. It was like a diagram of fishes of all different sizes, such as might be used to illustrate the principle of the food chain. This particular afternoon stands out because Senator Robert Byrd, in his youth a Klan sympathizer and in later years the majority leader of the U.S. Senate, whipped off the jacket of his five-hundred-dollar silk suit, and clambered up onto the flat bed of a truck. There, to attract the crowd for his speech, he put his fiddle to his chin and played "Turkey in the Straw." Played it like a statesman.

One reason for all the sneaking around was that San-dra's father (her mother had died long ago) didn't care for me, despite my respected position as a frequent obit-uarist. I had my suspicions about him as well, for he was a genuinely creepy character. His nose was covered in blackheads, giving it the look of a fresh strawberry, and his morals were such that they did no credit to the image of funeral directors or evangelists—nor of jewellers, for that matter. In his office in back of the funeral home, he dealt in secondhand rings—Knights of Columbus rings, signet rings, rings with monograms, rings with big stones. He displayed them in stacks of plush-lined trays, the kind in which the rings are protected from theft by a thin bar running down the centre of each row. A nice array of men's and women's watches, also accumulated during decades of stripping the bodies, was more or less a sideline. In an unsuccessful attempt to be nice to each other, I bought a fabulously expensive watch he offered me for only thirty dollars, but later I had to pawn it in New York when I'd run out of blood to sell to the blood bank, and was never in a position to redeem it.

I wasn't at the paper very long before I had an opportunity to play an insignificant part in covering a rather extraordinary story, the Bishop Pike affair. James A. Pike was an Episcopalian bishop or, to be precise, the Resigned Bishop of California. He had previously been the dean of St. John the Divine in New York, the world's largest cathedral (St. Peter's in Rome being technically a church, not a cathedral). But as he rose in the hierarchy, becoming one of the two or three best-known clergymen in the country, his relations with the church establishment grew fractious. The first incident was in the early 1950s when he'd refused to accept an honorary degree from an Episcopal university that didn't admit Blacks. From that point right up to the Vietnam War, he had engaged in a campaign of rebellious liberalism that seemed to be testing the social and in fact the ethical relevancy, not only of Episcopalians, but also of Christian denominations generally. Why only a year before he'd dared to ordain a woman, a known woman, as deacon of his diocese! The bishops assembled in woodsy seclusion at Oglebay Park in Wheeling to try him for heresy. My role was merely to supply some colour to the experienced reporters, but that's enough to allow me to brag of having covered a heresy trial. That's a distinction much rarer than merely to have studied this figure of the

1960s, who's forgotten now but was as important then as, say, Timothy Leary, and who died a few years later in true 1960s (and true biblical) fashion, while wandering in the desert in search of fulfilment.

My only other brush with the mighty was when Walter Reuther, the president of the United Auto Workers union, the architect of the merger of the AFL and the CIO, and the inventor of the sit-down strike, had his bodyguards throw me out of a funeral parlour. His father, Valentine Reuther, an ancient Wheeling radical who had once been a drayman for Schulbach's brewery and often ran for Congress as a socialist, had died. The famous and powerful son was to leave the bargaining table during an impending strike to attend the services, and I was to try to get a comment from him on the progress of the talks. I waited in the parking lot and tried to get his attention as he entered the building. Failing, I had no choice, it seemed, but to approach him in the chapel itself. One of his eyebrows flickered and two thugs in shiny suits put me back in the parking lot again. By luck more than good sense, I managed to reach him by phone later, just as he was leaving town, and got at least some quote, however feeble.

For the most part, though, I was inconspicuous, joyously so, even though I was omnipresent or tried to be. I was able to befriend bail bondsmen and rounders, occasionally stumbling on a feature story that called for a slight literary flair, as when I found an old miner back up in the hills behind the Ferry who had once played in one of the miners' marching bands. "In those days you had your Welshmen's band and your Pollack band and your German band and so on and so forth, and we got four dollars for every miner's funeral we played at and there was enough funerals to keep 'em working all the time."

I was trying to juggle these many different roles, to find my way as a writer while staying alive as a reporter, to remain on acceptable terms with Sergeant Icehouse Hixenbaugh at night while his colleagues trailed me during the day because I was subversive, to keep all my sets of acquaintances apart from one another, and my life compartmentalized. To be productive amid the chaos I had to keep moving all the time, literally day and night. In such a situation, one to which I would find myself reverting for long periods later in my life, I came to value whatever little bits of ritual the whirl of events allowed. One of these was an afternoon meal with some of the old newshounds each Thursday, once we had cashed our cheques at the publisher's bank. The sessions took place at a restaurant near the head of the Alley that hadn't been touched since the 1930s. The cast of diners changed slightly from week to week, but often included Ed Whelan, a man in his early fifties, whose moustache looked as though it had been drawn with a 4B pencil. His worst problem was alcoholism, but he also once had been an inmate of the federal drug addiction facility at Lexington, Kentucky, where he had known several important jazz figures. While the rest of us began to eat, he would put most of his pay into an envelope and send it to his wife in Cincinnati as the weekly instalment on his huge matrimonial debt. Then he would take off his hat—it wasn't a homburg but it had that same air of obsolete solidity. He would look at it and roll the brim up all the way round and then put it squarely back on his head and tell me about his problems.

He had been discharged from more papers than any-one else I've ever known or heard about. He was on his third or so swing through Wheeling and was desperately clinging to his position only through the affection of some older executives who went back to the days of Hard Cash Ogden himself. Whelan drank in long binges, which seemed to be touched off by almost anything. Before capital punishment was abolished, even before the electric chair, when convicts were hanged in the high concrete room in the penitentiary at Moundsville, a few miles downriver, it was the warden's custom to place bot-tles of good bourbon along the gallery desk so the reporters and legal witnesses could get some refreshment before the gruesome ceremony. Most would require more than a little such preparation. Sober observers said this was what the warden hoped for, so that the press wouldn't notice if the executioner misplaced the noose so that the victim slowly strangled instead of dying of a swift broken neck. After each hanging, I was told, Whe-lan would disappear for days, maybe weeks, not so much out of horror at the event, which he perhaps had not seen from beneath the table, but because the free bottles had reactivated his need. He would sometimes joke that he was "livin' on Jones Street."

As if that weren't bad enough, he was also an ex-con, and none the better for the experience. Seeing a licence plate was enough to set him off in a wave of harsh nos-talgia for the life in the institutions where he'd done time, latterly for taking a pot-shot at a clergyman with whose wife he had been fooling around. His own wife, out of disgust with his drinking as much as from a sense of estrangement due to his absence, had divorced him while he was inside and got custody of their son, who was now grown up and working for one of the wire services. Upon his release Mrs. Whelan had somehow won alimony or support payments retroactive to the start of his sentence.

All in all it was a pretty good joint, he was telling me one day in the restaurant. *Medium security, built for six hundred and with only maybe a thousand guys in it at the time. Everybody got all the beef they wanted and there was plenty of time to walk around on the work details every day. Lockdown every night, of course, four guys in a cell, they were big cells with two pairs of bunks and a head and sink. At first there were only three of us in this one cell, you see, but finally a young fellow transferred in and it came out that he couldn't write, didn't know how, and would I write to his wife for him? Well, this went on for weeks, months. He's telling me what to put in the letters and it's darling this and honey that. Later I find out the guy's in for incest with his twelve-year-old daughter. Here all the time he'd had me writing all this stuff to her. Well, word got out, of course. A con said to him in the rec yard, "I'd never fuck my own daughter, man, unless she was really worth it." Then he stabbed him.*

I was listening but he would have continued even if I hadn't paid attention. That's what he was like when he got caught up in one of his nightmare reveries. He was letting his meal go cold while I ploughed through mine.

Now OP in Columbus, that's a different matter. OP was the Ohio Penitentiary, a literary sort of place. O. Henry had done his time there. So had Chester Himes, the author of *Cotton Comes to Harlem* and other novels, who wrote of seeing two inmates stab each other to death in an argument over whether Paris was the capital of France or France the capital of Paris. *In OP you got forty-six-hundred and they're in the cell all the time except for haircuts every two weeks or the exercise yard or of course in the infirmary. There are people who fell there for nothin' at all, nothin'. I knew one guy, he was in for stealing copper pipe from the place he worked for, for god sake. Being such a student of the mortuary arts, I know you'll appreciate this one: some dumb undertaker put in a fake death certificate for himself so the insurance would pay off a fifteen-hundred-dollar car loan or something. Anyway, all of them seemed to get out eventually on parole or writs. Now the way it was with me was that I was there less than eighteen months and for the first year I got drunk once a week. Julep, they call it. Made from fruit juice, any kind of fruit juice. You make it or you buy it. Nobody's supposed to have more than one dollar at a time but of course everybody does. Lots of things used as a medium of exchange of course. One con paid money for the shit of white boys, so white boys' shit became a kind of money.* I made a face to remind him I was eating. *Sorry, kid. Anyway as I was saying I got out of there, parole, but for two years I wasn't even supposed to go into restaurants where hard stuff was served, not even poolrooms, not to mention that I couldn't leave the country if I'd wanted to. So really, when you come down to it, I figured I wasn't much better off than I was before except that now, outside, I knew that anything you get for free you can keep.*

It was at that point that I looked up and saw Father's friend Alec standing in the doorway, squinting as his eyes adjusted to the darkness. I sensed what the trouble was before the thought was articulated in the brain.

"I've got some bad news for you, son." The softness

in his voice was startling. "Your father's had a sick spell at the plant."

"Is it serious?" The question seemed to be coming from someone else.

"I'm afraid it is."

I was getting my coat from the hook. "He's dead, isn't he?" I asked.

"I'm afraid so, son." Again the gentleness from such a big rough man. "I'm sorry."

Alec had his car out front and we drove to the hospital on 20th Street. It was the hospital where I'd been born and it looked like a crumbling castle. Parts of it hung over the shelf that had been carved out of the hillside. We went down to the cellar. Mother was in the corridor in a state of near hysteria. She kept saying, "They've taken him from me, *they've* taken him from me!" Her sister Ruth motioned me to the morgue and pointed to the body lying on the gurney. We pulled back the sheet. He was wearing a plaid flannel work shirt and his lips were as blue as old denim. His eyelids seemed very thin, almost translucent.

I went back to the paper looking for Haven Thompson. I found him in the back shop, conferring with Winnie Winiesdorffer, one of the compositors, who was working at the stone. I told him what had happened and that I needed some time off. Later that night, after I'd seen the undertaker, I returned to the newsroom and wrote the obituary.

There was much to be done and I did most of it wrong. We notified the Red Cross, which contacted the navy, which granted my brother emergency leave to fly in from California, where he was stationed at the time.

Much to my embarrassment, Father had been a Freemason. This was fine for an English policeman, in my view, but demeaning in a parent, though I see now that he was only looking for companionship and that, once again, Mother ruined everything with her increasingly worrisome behaviour. In any event, Dale and I had both heard him say over the years that he should be buried wearing his Masonic apron, and so we supplied it to the undertaker when we took in his blue serge suit. But the sight of him wearing it there in his casket was a great affront to his fellow Masons, for, as I should have known, the apron is only to be used with official Masonic funerals, which this one wasn't. The screw-up was somehow typical.

Mother carried on wildly and those who came to pay their respects were for the most part chary of talking to her. In her first few days as a widow, she sold all her husband's tools and began throwing out photos of his parents. A year or so later, long after I had left, she had a tombstone put up over his grave. It bore the inscription

Step softly please
Here lies my soul mate
His constant and tender love
Shall forever light my way

which frankly I thought was a bit much in the circumstances. But I saw it for the first time more than ten years after the fact.

By then, Wheeling seemed to have disappeared almost totally. With the collapse of the American steel industry, the city lost at least half its population and

virtually all of its claim on urban-ness. The city I
remember was a late-modernist miniature, complete in
every detail, with a financial district, say, and a jewellery
district and a wholesale produce district. It was a big
city shrunk in scale. When I saw it next, downtown was
largely vacant, and arsonists who had nothing better to
do worked to make it seem even worse than it was.

Ironically, both Bethlehem and 29th Street were
destroyed in one swoop, by construction of one of the
last links in the nationwide system of Interstate highways, which President Eisenhower had initiated as a
means of evacuating the people during a communist
attack from the air. Even the mob had called it quits,
and eventually the authorities would finally succeed in
putting poor Paul Hankish, by then a seriously ill dia-
betic, away for life.

The city was returning to the frontier whence it
came. Deer started wandering down from the hills.
They quickly lost their fear and their numbers grew.
Wild turkey were next. The wilderness was getting its
health back perhaps. Vines were poised to start climbing up the monuments.

I could recognize a few buildings here and there.
There were even a few people still around I remembered, but they hated me for my political apostasy. I felt
that my personal past had vanished, been used up, been
consumed in a fire-storm, and I soon came to feel that
this was probably just as well.

But I've allowed myself to run ahead of the
narrative.

I was in New York now, living under the name A.J. Hand, trying to come to terms with recent events.

Father hadn't left any money, but in his last few months he had paid off the mortgage on the hate-filled little house in Bethlehem, and I got the impression that there were some unexpected windfall sums, small insurance policies from his employer and his union, perhaps even from the Freemasons. I wasn't certain Mother was capable of maximizing whatever resources there were. I proposed that together we make a full accounting, so we would know what our position was. We fell to arguing when she refused to share any information whatever. The quarrel was of course only a shorthand reference to her lifelong anger and also to my newfound sense, which I've needed years of thought and therapy to put behind me, that she was culpable in his death—the death of the only person who I never doubted for a moment loved me. I told her I would stay for twelve months, pay the bills from my newspaper salary (they consumed it) and help her in whatever other way I could. By the end of the given period, I figured, the money from the estate would either be gone or it wouldn't: whichever way would be a clear sign of the true situation. I never determined how much of her mourning was guilt or what portion of her grief was loneliness. I could see only that, without her foil, her temper deteriorated even further. I was hard put to avoid the gaping pit, and finally had to move out of the house.

I checked into the YMCA on 20th Street where a friend of mine lived who was talking about launching a little magazine (as with so many little magazines, one would need only the premiere issue in order to have a complete run). There was barely space in his room for the iron bed and the chest of drawers with cigarette burns all round the edge, much less for the portrait busts he'd been making. I found the Y a loudly congenial place, as it was about to go off, pending the day when methadone users would outnumber Methodists. At twenty-one dollars a week, however, the rent was more than I could afford. When one of the reporters at the *Intell* left town, I was able to assume her spot in a communal apartment in the old flat-iron building at Main and South Streets, between the newsroom and the cavernous railway freight sheds by the river. Five of us lived there for what one or two persons might have expected to pay for other accommodations of equivalent squalour. A determining factor in the price was the way that one could reach the place only by passing through the premises of the business that occupied the ground floor. The establishment was called the Stark Artificial Limb Company. We had latchkeys and at night would grope our way across the showroom in the dark, bumping into wooden legs and other such prostheses.

I marvel now at how busy I was and to so little purpose. No doubt it was partly to put emotional distance between Mother and myself that I ran everywhere and took part in everything, though beneath the desperation, I believe, was a real sense of joy at being able to indulge an appetite for experience. The war dominated the news and reaction to it was becoming the central element in the arts, whether boldly stated or not, and I entered into a stage, lasting perhaps a dozen years, when I felt completely attuned to the rhythms of the popular culture even though I was not a direct consumer of its goods. All through that period, for example, I never had a stereo or even a radio but knew all the new music intimately, as though some generational organ inside me had sucked it in from the atmosphere and drawn it through my pores. Looking back, I seem to have been balanced on the moment, living in past and present alike, nocturnally and in daylight. I was sick, frightened and disgusted most of the time, but strangely I was never more open to experience.

Through Mary Tominack I got to know Don West, a famous folk poet, the author of *Anger in the Land* and other chapbooks in the obsolete conventions: the son of a southern sharecropper, he was a far more important person than he was a writer. After studying in Sweden, he returned to America to open a racially integrated school designed to coax abilities out of students from throughout the Appalachians. Later, he defied death threats to help unionize the miners in Kentucky and the textile workers in North Carolina, and subsequently taught in Atlanta, where the state government fired him for his anti-segregationist views and the Ku Klux Klan burned his house. Later still, the McCarthy witch-hunters went after him. (How often I heard of those being attacked by the Klan also being pursued by the House Un-American Activities Committee, a convenient coincidence in the same manner as the Chicago mafia and the CIA working together to harass Castro.) Through Don in turn I met his daughter Hedy West, the folk-singer and songwriter who lived in England; from her exile she put me in touch with various people there, particularly after I promoted and did the advance work on a series of concerts she gave in the Wheeling area to benefit one arm of the Movement or the other. Working nights allowed me pretty free access to the newspaper's cameras and darkroom, which led me to photography, and I got to the point where some friends in the Movement put on an exhibit of my slumscapes at the Jesuit college. That in turn encouraged me to make small personal films. The first was small indeed, though Bill Forbes and Arthur Tarlow appeared in it, along with a girlfriend of the day, whose devoir was to run along the top of a retaining wall with her long hair trailing behind her as required by the script, which I made up as we went. Tarlow kept insisting that the film be called *Prometheus in Bondage*. The second one, I decided, should be more ambitious, and I began scrounging equipment and personnel. Among the volunteers I met Jasmine Erskine, who was two or three years older than I was.

I find it difficult to describe her without using the word *very*. She was very attractive, with a sort of butterscotch complexion, and very smart and very funny, very rebellious towards authority, and very committed to politics, being the child of wealthy liberal parents who, though divorced, were united in seeing opposition to the war as part of a continuum that also included the New Deal. It wasn't long after volunteering her services that she pronounced my filmmaking silly and drew me into her own world of personal expression, a plexus of painting, found sculpture and assemblage. One day at an abandoned building I happened on a wonderful wooden sign, as weathered as some old hobo's face. Large red letters had once said POSITIVELY NO TRESPASSING but only the first word still remained. I carried it around with me for months as all-purpose statement, as a pet almost, finding it an adjoining seat in restaurants and at the theatre. Nothing further needed to be said.

Jasmine's father was a physician who, in addition to his medical practice, operated a clinic where well-heeled alcoholics could dry out in a bucolic setting. Over the years the business had made him as wealthy as any of his patients, and Jasmine had been reared in an up-to-date kind of opulence that left me, in my first brush with prosperity, ill at ease. She was quick to put down my obvious discomfort and just as quick to trivialize her advantages, but that did little to improve my situation and had the effect, I believe, of increasing the attraction I felt, which was dangerously unrequited even when she was at her most passionate. Dr. Erskine was perplexed by all this, as he must have been by all her male friends, whom he tended to mistake for one another. He was a big man with a bald bullet-shaped head and no neck, somewhat in the manner of Erich von Stroheim. Silver-framed spectacles only added to the general air of metallurgy that contradicted his expansive cordiality in most matters except his daughter's moral welfare. He was extremely proud of his richly panelled den, where by pressing buttons he could make a complete bar appear from behind one wall. "Come on in here, boy," he would say, grabbing my shoulder. "I want to introduce you to a couple friends of mine. Jack Daniels and Johnny Walker." Her mother had remarried and lived in New York and Jasmine, it was understood, would join her there next autumn when she started NYU. An odd choice, that, for her father, I'm fairly certain, had gone to Columbia and she had the money and the grades to study wherever she pleased, but typical of her also. Until then she was putting in her time at Bethany College, a local private school, where she somehow got me a meal ticket to the cafeteria so that I could keep up my caloric intake.

The doctor always seemed to be at home, and I had a growing number of roommates who came and went at all hours. These facts went together to force Jasmine and me to make love at unusual times and in even stranger places, though this was very much her preference. She enjoyed a thin blade of danger to heighten the excitement. The need may have been a family trait, as her father, it seemed to me, liked to see how close he could come to alcoholism without erasing the line that separated him from his clientele. On one occasion, she and I undressed each other within sight of him, or what would have been in sight of him had he not fallen asleep in a deep leather chair with a crystal decanter at his elbow. That time, I believe, we risked homicide, for he was especially protective of his remarkable daughter, particularly given the guilt he felt at the divorce.

Her eroticism was so extreme and yet so offhand: that's half of what made her irresistible. It was as though she were possessed of wonderful arcane knowledge that it is given only a few people to have—alchemy, perhaps, or a mastery of some delicate surgical procedure—that bored her to tears except at the precise moment it was being put at the service of a memorable cause. She reserved much of her intensity for art, about which she was in fact downright profligate in her love (that was the other part of the attraction). I've never forgotten a day we spent walking through the Carnegie International at Pittsburgh where her brilliant impromptu comments drew a small crowd. The people followed us around the gallery from room to room, huddling just within earshot, and all the while Jasmine remained oblivious to them, showing a combination of scrutiny and myopia that was altogether characteristic. I suppose that like those eavesdroppers I was always courting condescension to associate with persons who were smarter than I was. Only by that method could I create an environment in which I felt I was developing whatever talent or ideas might have got trapped inside me somehow.

I was determined to save myself from the vacuousness that was all around me as well as from the hatred and violence. I wasn't proficient at articulating my ideas even to myself, and that's always a much easier proposition than transmitting them; but I did know in so many words what the larger difficulty appeared to be. The problem was not the war, the problem was America. For some time I had been nurturing a plan. Now with Jasmine I had an escape route as well.

The stated period during which I had promised Mother that I would remain close to her side was drawing to an end. As the deadline approached, she became more imaginative in her denunciations, daring me to leave as she damned me to hell. One night I went into her room and found her sitting up in bed scowling. I've come to say goodbye, I said. She was distant but not actually hostile.

I left.

Jasmine's mother, a stylish and well-coiffed woman, lived with her second husband in a spacious apartment at Fifty-eighth and Lex that was full of expensive art and heavy ornaments. She seemed to feel that Jasmine's interest in me could be explained only in terms of my being a collectible. She had extra bedrooms galore and insisted that Jasmine live there with her and her step-father while going to university. It did make economic sense. I knew what the housing problem was like, for I was sharing a place on Avenue A near Tompkins Square, where each morning the discarded syringes lay thick as walnuts on the ground. The ancient rooms were high but narrow, with mould forming on the outside walls, and the corners were full of stuff that lay unclaimed since the time whoever owned it had died or been sent to Riker's Island. But Jasmine and I were together every day when she came down to Washington Square for classes.

In those days Greenwich Village was still a flourishing enterprise, though it had taken a rough turn. Walking up and down, huddled inside a reefer-coat from the army surplus store, you got somewhat the same feeling you get in England, that history lies in layers beneath your feet. The past was almost tactile but it wasn't real. What set it apart was its improbable innocence. Whether you looked at the residue of the First World War generation of writers or the atmosphere that Dylan had bequeathed to his folk-singing friends in 1963 or so, you couldn't help being brought up short by the light-ness and optimism that had vanished somehow, been killed off by the new realities. One of these was the occu-pation of the East Village. It didn't have the same artistic history—until relatively recently it had been part of the Lower East Side of Italian and Jewish immigrants—and there was nothing to give it the hard centre of cultural humanism so apparent in the other, which people were beginning to call the West Village. The New Wave was under way there. You could see it in the rejection of gentleness and in the violence that informed the happenings, the light shows and most of all the street life.

I had a routine because I had a mission. Each morning, before the lack of sleep disabled me, I would ascend Fifth Avenue to the main public library at Forty-second Street and study the Canadiana there. It wasn't all in one place but it amounted to an extraordinary collection. Since the day Mary Tominack first put the notion of Canada in my head, I had been subscribing to Canadian periodicals and through Jasmine's example monitoring the CBC. In time I got to the point of maintaining a correspondence with a few Canadian writers. Now, sitting in the library, sometimes taking pills to help me stay awake in the impossibly overheated reading room, I deepened my commitment to learning Canadian politics, economics, culture—the works. The abiding tradition of anti-Americanism, always present deep down in the lay public if not always pursued by cowardly governments, was one I found especially attractive, though I was careful not to let my own enthusiasms shape my curriculum. For the only time in my life, I was a serious pupil in addition to being a good student.

Jasmine's commuting schedule, from uptown to downtown, from downtown to uptown, allowed her to get lost along the way by the simple expedient of disappearing at the bottom of the loop. At the end of the day, when I had returned bleary-eyed from the library, she would vanish conveniently from Washington Square to reposition herself in the area around St. Mark's Place. W.H. Auden lived somewhere along that street, but we never saw him; he would have been incongruous to say the least among the poets who did hang out there, such as Ray Bremser, with his famous mumble, or Ted Berrigan, or Joel Oppenheimer, the leading figure of that day and place.

It was not easy to forget that there was a war on. The city was polarized, and our group certainly, and perhaps the opposing one as well, sought safety in numbers. Yet there was no community as such, the way there surely had been in the West Village for so long. People cultivated a secondhand appearance and lived a secondhand aesthetic but without any reference to what had gone before (in clear contrast to the style that the Beatles were setting at the time). There was a metallic edge to people's lives that prevented intimacy with either past or present. To be high all the time was the ideal, but it seemed to me to be based on the recognition of despair, not the search for joy or peace or even excitement. New York had lost touch with the vernacular in itself. Living there, at least in circumstances such as ours, was like subsisting everyday on soup that tasted only of chemicals. The feeling wasn't remotely so strong with Jasmine as it was with me, however.

The centre of disrespectable literary life was the Peace Eye Bookstore on East 10th Street between B and C. Hebrew letters on the window, left over from the days when a butcher shop had occupied the premises, attested to the fact that the establishment was kosher, which it most certainly no longer was even in a metaphorical sense. In the front room the proprietor, Ed Sanders, a fiercely intelligent drug-culture poet with a degree in Egyptology, had arranged unusual paperbacks under thematic headings of his own devising, such as *glop* and *slupe*. Mementos lined the walls. A photograph reminds me that he had the famous sandwich board that Allen Ginsberg, now an East 10th Street neighbour, had worn at a seminal demonstration in 1964: the one with the words POT IS FUN in huge black letters. Sanders also sold genuine Allen Ginsberg pubic hairs, packaged individually in the type of glassine envelopes used by philatelists. In the back room sat the mimeograph machine on which Sanders produced his literary journal, *fuck you / a magazine of the arts*. I found him a cynical and distant figure, quite the opposite of his collaborator, Tuli Kupferberg.

Tuli, who has always looked younger than his years though he's perpetually haggard, had been around the Village for long enough to have known Max Bodenheim (murdered in 1954) and other hold-overs from the twenties. He was and has continued to be a poet of singular originality, publishing most of his material himself (in those days, as Birth Press, an imprint he used on mimeographed books which he then gave away). I once saw him react to some unwittingly surrealistic utterance by a child of perhaps two, in such a way that his whole body and spirit seemed to give in to laughter. He and Sanders, along with a third man, Ken Weaver, a drummer, a round and silent presence whose long straight hair was like the inversion of his enormous beard, had teamed up as a group called the Fugs, originally the

Village Fugs—*fug* being the word that Norman Mailer's publisher had forced him to use in *The Naked and the Dead* in place of *fuck*. The band was one of the important protest instruments of the sixties. Tuli, who was capable of writing a beautiful art song as well as, more typically, "Johnny Piss-Off Meets the Red Baron," provided most of their material (the rest was adapted from Blake). I learned only years later that Tuli was the person Ginsberg described in *Howl* who "jumped off the Brooklyn Bridge this actually happened and walked away unknown and forgotten into the ghostly daze of Chinatown soup alleys & firetrucks not even one free beer." Except that it wasn't the Brooklyn Bridge but the Manhattan Bridge (Allen's memory was often loose with such details). I once had the honour of performing with the Fugs on stage. While Tuli and Ed sang one of their standards, I paraded about with a placard bearing the slogan FUCK FOR PEACE or some other platitude of the day.

For a time I took up with a street-theatre group called Teatro de Tripas, the gut theatre. We practised a primitive form of performance art, such as when we stood at busy intersections dressed in old tuxedos and gave public readings from *TV Guide* in English and Spanish while smashing television sets with a stolen fire axe. I hid out in my Canadian studies during the day but was drawn at night into an ever more bizarre world of jagged nerves and wino cafeterias. I was sick much of the time with bronchitis that in my ignorance I thought was congenital but that turned out to be more sartorial: I didn't have a coat that buttoned up to the neck and lacked the means of getting one.

Jasmine and I were growing apart as we learned more about each other. She didn't believe that the nihilist mood was at base concerned with the absence of humanity all around us, and I suppose I was contemptuous of the comfortable position from which she in her own way protested the war, a way different from mine though of course just as valid. In any case, the war was the proper metaphor for our relationship as it was for everything. I got in deeper and feared what withdrawal might do to me and so could only become even more involved than before. As I did so, I grew even to dislike her and was repaid in kind. Yet we stayed together, with mutual morbid fascination slowly taking the place of shared affection. It was the Vietnam of love affairs all right. It took time, though, before I could admit to myself what I had been forced to conclude: that beneath it all, she was an American, she was infected with the great American virus, that love was just as impossible there as any other worthwhile impulse, state or endeavour, all of them rendered unworkable by the institutionalized violence, the purblind worship of stupidity and all the rest. I felt I could never again have a serious intimate relationship with an American, and I have not.

These matters seemed like the great revelations of my young life up to that time, yet I find it difficult to express them with the intensity of that moment, now that I have lived with them so long. What did America feel like then, what did it seem to be?

In 1966 I thought that Americans were the salt of the earth: and so wherever they walked, nothing would ever grow again. What was most astounding was their hard

shell of ignorance that seemed to preclude any acknowl-
edgement of guilt. And they had so much to be guilty
for. The business of America, Calvin Coolidge's remark
to the contrary, was not just business, it was everybody
else's business, an attitude that inevitably led to violence. There were clear historical reasons for it. The
whole notion of the frontier in its boundlessness combined with the calvinist heritage to create a religion of
conscious destruction. The people had no connected-
ness to say the least, and they took their chaos with
them wherever they went. It produced a kind of evil.
Murder was how these folks showed affection. I
wouldn't have been surprised if Death actually turned
out to be an American. "Mr. William T. (Bill) Death Jr.
at your service," he'd say in some flat, nasal accent.
"Death's the name and death's the game."

"Is there good money in that?" you would be
expected to ask, shaking his bony hand.

"Well, I'm comfortable."

America with all its apocalyptic furniture! The point
wasn't simply that every night was Hallowe'en for real.
It was that everyone was on moral disability. LAND OF
MUTANTS should have been the motto on the licence
plates. Since 1820, when fairly accurate records started
to be kept, about fifty-two million people had immi-
grated to the U.S. As far as I was concerned, they were
all wrong to have come. It's all a big mistake, I would
have said to them. Go back and face the czar or the des-
iccated potatoes. It's one big joke, the oldest and cruellest joke in the world—if you buy the premise, you
buy the punchline. The great experiment, they called it.
But the experiment failed, nothing good was proved,

the laboratory exploded and the stench of rotten eggs
and sulphur pervaded everything. Emerson said that
being an American was not a nationality as such but a
moral condition. He was close. It is an immoral condition. The line between genealogy and criminology got
mighty blurry sometimes.

No one was contending that one government was
necessarily any better than another in its potential for
good or disposition towards evil (by this time I'd discovered George Woodcock). Some are simply worse, more
vicious, more stupid, wholly owned subsidiaries of the
devil, because they mirror the culture, in the broadest
sense, that supports them. Yet, perversely and tri-
umphantly, it's only in their culture that one society
sometimes expresses qualities that transcend their governments and their businessmen and so help compensate for them. What was the real reason all those men in
the Top Hat had fought the Nazis?, I wanted to ask.
Surely not revulsion at malevolence and worse, more a
question of rivalry, of hating the Germans' education
and wanting to destroy Britain economically. As forever
unfathomable as the Holocaust seemed, it was, to us,
equally incomprehensible that a deed so evil could have
escaped somehow being America's fault, at least in part.
Everything was calculated violence and spontaneous
greed. There was no moral commitment because there
was no civilization worth the name, and no civilization
because there was no education, no humaneness, no
sense of the necessity of ongoing improvement, except
in a few brave and isolated people, saintly really, whose
lives showed what culture really was. It was always
shocking to discover such a person since the majority

stated the problem so convincingly and with such apparent unanimity. You could see Americans returning to their roots, with their pop culture superstitions and their television cabbala. It was only a question of time until grave goods came back into fashion and the dead would be buried with their credit cards and small appliances, sitting upright in Fords and Chevs, facing east, towards Wall Street and the Pentagon.

I found it a constant struggle to keep out the terror and let the stimulation enter. It proved impossible, in fact. Some days the history would rise in the gorge like vomit, then go down slowly with my thoughts of escape. One had to remove oneself to avoid being contaminated. One had to resign. My only ambition now was to be a last-generation American and a first-generation Canadian.

"Did you grow up in the States?" somebody would be sure to ask.

"No one in the States grows up. That's the problem."

Under the Canadian Immigration Act in force at the time, you had to be eighteen in order to enter Canada permanently. I had turned eighteen now.

"Why did you come to Canada?" people might enquire.

"Privacy," I would tell them.

But all the while I was saying something quite different to myself. First the border formalities loomed and then, after a short time, they receded. *Fuck you America,* I was screaming silently. *Have a nice day.*

CHAPTER THREE

FINE ICONIC BOOKS
AND DEEP
COMBATIVE EGOS

A FEW MONTHS before I took up permanent residence in Toronto in 1967, two young English professors met to establish a small publishing house, an
event that would have great significance for the Canadian book world and coincidentally for me as well. Legend, which was soon to encrust the people and
happenings I am about to describe, once insisted that
the founding took place over beer at the Bay-Bloor Tavern of blessed memory. In any event, the principals were
David Godfrey and Dennis Lee, figures with quite different sensibilities who soon came to be the separate
halves of an enterprise that was better known and more
complex than its individual components. It was called
House of Anansi Press, or at least that was the style for
all but the first printing of the first book, Dennis's collection of poetry, *Kingdom of Absence*, whose title page
spelled the name Ananse. Both renderings were acceptable for the spider-god and trickster found in African
and Caribbean folklore. As far as I'm aware, however,

neither had any special relevance to the little basement publishing firm except that Dave Godfrey, like so many other young liberals, had been in CUSO, or Canadian University Service Overseas, doing volunteer labour in the Third World. In his case that meant teaching school in West Africa (while also, it was said, playing trumpet in a group called the Gold Coast Jazz and High Life Band). So stated the oral equivalent of his curriculum vitae and hence the African name.

Dave, who was twenty-nine when I first met him, was bamboo-slender with a prognathous chin and a great deal of brown hair that was at once both straight and unruly. He moved everywhere in a bright haze of nervous energy, as though surrounded by some strange electromagnetic field. This condition allowed him to work simultaneously on an extraordinary number of projects and causes, at least for short periods. It also contributed to his mystery, which was already considerable. He was a Winnipeger by birth but got all his education, undergraduate and otherwise, in the States. He was one of those students whose literary promise had always impressed people, or so Wallace Stegner, who had been one of his instructors at Stanford, told me years later. Now he was teaching English at Trinity College and pursuing a variety of nationalistic missions and keeping up a prodigious output of writing, including proto-postmodernist short stories with outdoor settings. These were appearing in *Saturday Night* disguised as a sports column, with the helpful connivance of the magazine's managing editor, Kildare Dobbs (with whom Dave would soon sever relations and attack in Picquefort's Column, a pseudonymous department he conducted in the *Canadian Forum*).

While at Stanford, Dave had met his wife, Ellen, whom rumour made the daughter of an important Illinois industrialist—accurately so, I believe. She seemed friendly but most proper and reserved, and so I was surprised one day when she told me that she had once dated Neal Cassady, the mythic wild man after whom Jack Kerouac had patterned Dean Moriarty in *On the Road*. The Godfreys were living at 671 Spadina Avenue, in an impressive Edwardian house they rented from the university, which counted a few such gems among all the slum properties that otherwise made up its extensive real-estate portfolio. I had exchanged a letter or two with Dennis Lee and so knew about Anansi, but I hadn't actually met him and was slow to make contact after arriving in town during a crystalline blizzard. Perhaps a couple of weeks passed before I telephoned one day and spoke to Dave, who invited me over.

He gave me the tour. It started in the garret, which he rented to a student from Ghana whom he introduced as Kwame John. It concluded in the cellar, one end of which had been converted to an office while another area, a furnace room set off by partitions, was shelved for the inventory of Anansi books.

At this point Anansi had published only a few titles in addition to *Kingdom of Absence*, the long meditative poem that Dennis had written in England five years earlier and whose failure to find a publisher, they said, was what prompted the two of them to go into business for themselves. There were also poetry chapbooks by Barry Charles and Janis Rapoport, two extremely young writers who prefigured Dennis's interest in people at the first stage of their careers (after which he often lost interest in them). The press had just received its first Canada Council grant to pursue a more professional programme, which included a new edition of *Absence* as well as three other books. Two were poetry: *The Absolute Smile* by George Jonas, the urbane Hungarian emigré, and *The Circle Game* by Margaret Atwood, who was more or less unknown, though the Contact Press edition of the book had won the Governor General's Award after its 250 copies had sold out. The other book was *Death Goes Better with Coca-Cola*, the collection of Dave's wonderfully anti-American short fiction from *Saturday Night* and elsewhere.

"This is it," Dave said with impatient pride.

I said it was an attractive set-up, or words to that effect.

Some bustling was evident upstairs on the ground floor, with heavy suitcases being bounced down the steps one at a time.

"Ellen and I have to go to Chicago for a couple of weeks. Do you have any place to stay?" I confessed that I hadn't. "You can stay here until we get back if you'll look after filling the orders as they come in." He showed me the system for invoicing, which I forgot almost immediately, and then they were off, whisked away in the middle of a commotion, the sort that always seemed to attend Dave's movements.

Dennis Lee never turned up. In fact, we didn't meet until some while later, once Dave had returned and hired me as Anansi's first full-time employee—for thirty-five dollars a week, fifteen of which I then kicked back to him in rent for the attic room I was to share with Kwame John.

It seemed just a little incongruous that Dave was teaching at Trinity. As far as anybody knew, he was not an Anglican—word was that he had converted to Judaism or was about to—but more importantly he was not what might be called an Anglican type. He was an entrepreneur. An entrepreneur of ideas at the moment but, in theory, of anything, as later events would prove. His nationalistic hatred of America was based on disillusionment and ultimately repulsion during his own experiences there. Dennis, when I finally got to know him, was quite different. His cultural compass had pointed across the Atlantic before the needle swung about to show him the way back home. He taught at Vic, which seemed perfect, for he was the heir to a staunch kind of middle-class suburban Methodism, most of whose adherents no doubt considered him an apostate because he had grown up to be an intellectual. He was secretly drawn to the Quakers as well as to the other extreme, though I suspect he feared that High Church people were looking down on him. One never knew for certain, for it was impossible to penetrate his wry cordiality without striking condescension. That is to say, he had the congenial manner of someone to whom the quality did not come naturally but had been made a habit though constant vigilance until it finally became permanent.

He was twenty-eight, with an enormous domed forehead stuffed with English literature and social conscience. He sported a little blond goatee and usually wore *djiskais*; he chain-smoked small cigars with plastic mouthpieces and gave the impression of fighting hard against the constriction and shrinkage that a certain type of WASP likes to write novels of rebellion about. He had yet to publish any of the children's verse that he had begun writing for his own kids, but it was certainly clear even then that the high culture in which he was schooled was always warring inside him with the popular culture from which he felt cut off. You can see the tension in the diction of his serious poetry and other work and hear it in the way he talked, with great precision and joy in language, but also with a gentle mockery that was a kind of reaching out. He was trying to teach himself quantum mechanics at night, and he played the piano, loudly and in the key of C. He spoke of Martin Heidegger and Al Purdy volubly and with almost equal reverence. I quickly made myself a disciple, or tried to; there were few places available and a great many applicants.

George Woodcock was right when he wrote in a letter to Dennis that "something unprecedented happened to Canadian publishing and even to Canadian writing when Anansi came on the scene." And indeed whenever I hold them in my hands today in second-hand book shops, I'm reminded how fresh and sophisticated, how powerful and, yes, how revolutionary the old Anansi titles seemed. As examples of bookmaking, they may also have been incredibly amateurish and naive, but in turning the obsolete pages, I always find preserved some suggestion of what the period was like. During the Centennial and for a couple of years afterwards, Anansi was at the forefront of a movement that it both helped to create and then gave voice to. There were many other little presses, of course, most of them personal vehicles for their editors, transient and homeopathic, but with some genuine place in the long equation of literature. Anansi was different. It was out to change writing by displacing the old generation with the new: the same implied function that the Hogarth Press or Boni and Liveright had voiced in their own day, with the same cocky self-assurance. In the process, though, Anansi actually wanted to change publishing as well, and to that end it was more successful.

Barring only Jack McClelland, who once gave Anansi a prognosis of six months, Canadian publishers were insufficiently interested in the new writers who were turning up in large numbers, driven, so it seemed at the time, by some great consensual imperative. Macmillian and Ryerson and Clarke, Irwin and Oxford and the University of Toronto Press all brought out Canadian books, but they seemed to Dennis to be unadventurous affairs, the inevitable result, so Dave, I believe, must have imagined, of the cautious corporatism or institutional restraint with which houses like that were burdened. McClelland was a separate case. He was a corporate showman, using his talent for ballyhoo to make a few select authors into public personalities, a process that included career-long commitments to promoting them and their works, both current and backlist. To Dave, who saw publishing as a political act, and Dennis, to whom it was a moral one, such behaviour, though fascinating, was abhorrent. In any event, it was often said that McClelland's skill as a talent scout had deteriorated. The youngest of his stars (of the ones whose shine persisted) was Leonard Cohen, who was past thirty-five and had defected to the States. Dennis once publicly compared Cohen's work more or less unfavourably with that of Bliss Carman.

Anansi was small in sales volume but big in its goals. Its main ambition, as seemed obvious even then, was to publish its own people, the ones engaged in the expression of a new Canadian reality, urban, politically savvy and "freewheeling" (Dennis's favourite word at the moment), and propel them into the mainstream. The place seemed haphazardly run, with erratic schedules, inconsistent design, almost non-existent promotion. Yet we were the new attractions at the zoo, drawing large crowds, and the media had to pay close attention even though they had never seen such animals before. Incredible though this may sound today, the big newspapers rushed to do full-page stories on us.

A few other small presses on the scene were engaged in interesting publishing too. Talonbooks was in the process of emerging from *Talon*, the little magazine, and there was another Vancouver press of some importance: Very Stone House, which the poets Patrick Lane and Seymour Mayne had started in 1966. But Very Stone House tapered off after a while, as Pat roamed restlessly around the country, haunted in some measure, I think, by the tragically early death of his elder brother, the poet Red Lane. Towards the end, their publications were chapbooks or folded broadsides under the imprint Very Stone House in Transit, put out from wherever Pat happened to be—logging in B.C. somewhere or hunting in the Rockies.

The most important underground press prior to Anansi had started in 1965 when Stan Bevington and a number of others had opened Coach House Press in Toronto, on Bathurst Street below Dundas, in a perfectly nice slum, which an overly officious city government later razed for a park. One approached the eponymous coach house by navigating a muddy little alley running beside a deserted building that had once been a locksmith's shop. Bevington, a printer, had red hair and wore a big beard, and was friendly in a slow-moving non-specific way—and equally so to everyone, in a style then associated with the young generation of British Columbians. His interest was in handsetting type and keeping his old Linotype in operating condition. The Coach House logo, then and later, was a cast-iron platen press with an enormous fly-wheel, and in those days they actually printed on the press from which the image had been made. Later, in the 1970s, Bevington made a complete volte-face, suddenly abandoning the traditions of the craft for the vanguard of computer-generated graphic arts. The switch was probably coincidental to the emergence of Coach House as one of the primary institutions of what would later be the prevailing orthodoxy, but the two events were parallel in time.

Bevington was a craftsman and designer, not a literary person, and had always looked to a variety of writers to work out among themselves what he should be printing. One of the earliest was bp Nichol, whose *Journeying & the Returns*, which I remember being excited about when it came out in 1967, was among the most imaginative of their works: a box containing a chapbook, an envelope of poems on individual cards, a flipbook that one fanned with one's thumb: all sorts of different work forms, including a plastic phonograph record of the author chanting. At one point, some of the Coach House poetry books were designed deliberately to make the poetry almost unreadable on the page—silver type on purple paper, that kind of thing. For some years, as a hallmark of their quality, the books all carried the motto "Printed in Canada by Mindless Acid FreaKs."

That's when Coach House was on the outside, knocking to be let in. Later (in retrospect, rather quickly) it became one of the most important pieces of infrastructure in the all-important Vancouver-Toronto axis that had sprung out of the old journal *Tish* and the Vancouver Poetry Conference of 1963: the Canadian members of the Black Mountain school as they were then thought of, later known as the language poets, the postmodernists. They were a cliquish bunch, a complete and almost closed society of theorists as well as prose writers and poets who, by the deadly serious late 1970s, had come to the top of Canadian literature. This was because they controlled much of the critical machinery, with *Open Letter* and many other journals, and what they wrote eventually became the dominant mode in English departments, particularly in those west of the Quebec-Ontario border.

But back in 1967, small press books sold hundreds of copies, not thousands; they didn't get reviewed in the *Globe and Mail* or stocked by Coles or the independent shops or the all-important department stores. And no writer ever made a proper career in small presses without graduating to more commercial ones. Anansi is important partly because it changed all that, at least for a time.

My grandfather, Herschel Fetherling: engineer, entrepreneur, amateur orientalist and collector of murder weapons. His financial ruin in the 1929 stock market crash brought about the family's expulsion from the upper middle class.

My English grandmother, Ethel Fetherling, fresh out of a European finishing school. She would come to a bad end in America, working as a hotel laundress well into her seventies and only narrowly escaping a grave in potter's field.

LEFT: "Remarkable for his Welsh-ness," my maternal grandfather, Owen Jones, far younger—and more cheerful—than I can remember him. He was by turns a boxer, steel-worker, farmer, beer-salesman and saloon-keeper. "Like Aldous Huxley, of whom he most assuredly never heard, he died on the day that President Kennedy was shot and was thus shortchanged in the amount of space the news of his passing was accorded in the papers."

BELOW: My parents, George and Mary Emma Fetherling, night-clubbing in 1941. He was 26, more than halfway through his short unhappy life; she was 30 and beginning to show signs of the mental and emotional instability that would damage everyone around her.

The author, holding a piece of found sculpture, at the entrance
to Newsboy Alley in 1966. The photograph was taken
by the redoubtable Jasmine Erskine.

The original home of House of Anansi Press as it looked in 1968, the year after the revolutionary publishing firm was founded by David Godfrey and Dennis Lee, with the author as its first full-time employee. *(Photo by Stan Bevington)*

LEFT: Rochdale College, the 18-storey educational experiment (and internationally infamous drug supermarket) under construction not far from Anansi. "I would chart the progress as I walked along Bloor Street every day." A photo by the author, taken in February 1968.

BELOW: The author and Allen Ginsberg in Toronto, 1968.

Gwendolyn MacEwen at the Royal Ontario Museum in 1968.
(Photo by Mac Reynolds)

Bill Kimber, looking every inch the sixties artist and illustrator. The place I shared with him and Elizabeth Woods on Church Street turned into a salon that became famous in Toronto underground circles: part literary drop-in centre, part intellectual after-hours joint. *(Photo courtesy of Bill Kimber)*

On a number of occasions, Anansi may have published some Coach House writers such as George Bowering, but the two presses were fundamentally different.
There was no unspoken Anansi manifesto, beyond a
kind of vague literary liberalism that was more of a sensibility than a philosophy (and in any case didn't necessarily even seem liberal some of the time). Anansi
writers tended to be tortured by some enemy whose
name they couldn't agree on. Dennis Lee spoke of
absence as the fact of cosmology brought home to daily
living. George Grant (one of Dennis's mentors) cited
technological empire as the problem. Charles Taylor, the
former China correspondent (and a Grant protégé by
way of Dennis), wrote of *radical Toryism* as the solution,
while Margaret Atwood, for her part, was characteristi-
cally the most forthright and unambiguous in locating
the villain somewhere between patriarchy as a social system and maleness considered as a pathological condition. In fact, it seemed to me with certainty then, and
still seems to me even now, that they were all, at some
fundamental level, against more or less the same thing:
Americanism, with its republican brutality and hatred
of culture. I wasn't an important writer but I found a
great sense of discovery in locating a group of people
who hated the same enemy I did (even if, because I had
been born there, they sometimes found it necessary to
hate me in the bargain).

Such was my private interpretation. But there was
no Anansi school in any sort of literary sense whatever.
There weren't even many authors who stayed with
Anansi for book after book. Dennis had a few generic
enthusiasms like anybody else—he was always a sucker

for a certain kind of ironic diction that was just on the verge of going bad in the fridge and turning into curdled surrealism—but he was remarkably broad-minded and catholic. This, I believe, was his true strength as an editor, rather than his ability as a talent-scout of unpublished writers, a gift much vaunted in what's written about him but which time has not necessarily confirmed.

In any case, Coach House was originally about craft and then about taking over the Can lit agenda and making what was previously unappreciated the standard curriculum. In that way, it must forever be a more important press than Anansi, which never had much sense of the book arts and led to developments in publishing more than to developments in literature as such. What it did manage to do, however, was to put a lot of new writers into the hands of the existing readership that didn't know about them. Often this was because no one else knew of them either (Anansi published an extraordinary number of first books, including my own). Sometimes, though, it was a matter of Anansi, with its flair for publicity, propelling a writer's career by pushing the *second* book, making the person a figure of public discussion. This was the case with, for example, Marian Engel. Her first book was *No Clouds of Glory* (a poor choice of title, I always thought—like a romance novel's—but forced on her by Longmans, a mainstream branch-plant house of the day). Anansi published her next one, *The Honeyman Festival*, which I still find the most satisfying and most whole of her works (though admittedly it was not so ambitious as some that followed); it was also the one that started to give her a place as a feminist writer. No one knew it at the time, but the most important intellectual figure whose first book bore the Anansi name was Michael Ignatieff. The book, which he co-edited, was a collection of papers on religion. Sounds terribly dull, but it derived from the first annual "international teach-in" held at the U of T and betrays Dennis's interest in educational reform, a subject that, in a way, would help shape Anansi's rise.

To say the least, Anansi had low overhead. In these early days especially, it sold a great deal through direct mail and by phone, though this was the result of fumbling, not mastery of any marketing techniques; and the house benefited from tremendous word-of-mouth and other automatic publicity. Because it was small and swift, it didn't need much infrastructure, and this seemed baffling to the Canadian trade publishers of those days, who, typically, had large staffs and published modest Canadian lists from the profits of the agency agreements under which they represented foreign publishers' lines in Canada. If Coach House was first about craft and printing the work of a few friends and later about technology and controlling the academic agenda, then Anansi was only ever about one thing: publishing. That was its genius really, and the soul of its expedient amateurism—something which career publishers found perplexing. Marsh Jeanneret of the University of Toronto Press once said to Dennis: "You mean to say that you people publish these *paperback books* [the italics were like tongs for picking up a disgusting object] with dirty words in them and they're reviewed in the *Globe and Mail* and sold at Britnell's?" He was genuinely mystified. We were thrilled.

We were also exhausted most of the time, and not infrequently on edge. I remember typing some letters for Dave one afternoon. One was to Charles Wright, the *New Yorker* poet with whom he had become friendly at one or another of his U.S. campuses—the University of Iowa, I believe. With publication of *The Dream Animal* in 1968, Wright became Anansi's token resident American on the list (until I acquired a manuscript for us from Allen Ginsberg), and Dave later published another of Wright's collections once he moved on to his next publishing venture. Anyway, Dave was telling him by mail what was happening to Anansi, how ten books had become twenty and then forty, and how more people were coming to work there all the time, how some days the place appeared to be operating twenty-four hours—and how, Dave wrote with a note of desperation, *all this is going on in the basement of my house!* In this case, the italics were those of disbelief.

———

As our books started to take hold and Anansi became famous as the apotheosis of underground, a steady procession of would-be authors, antagonists, job-seekers and potential hangers-on began knocking on the front door of No. 671, ignoring the printed notice urging them not to do so, and sometimes giving poor Ellen Godfrey reason to doubt our sanity or at least our moral probity. They would be instructed to go around the corner to Sussex Avenue, down a laneway and through the old walled garden full of weeds and children's toys. There they found a low doorway that gave onto a laundry room. Beyond that was the pathetic little hooch that I had made for myself after vacating the attic and leaving Kwame John in peace. It was a space about the size of a generous prison cell, which I shared with the furnace and the furnace pipes. My only piece of furniture was an old cot; I would unfold it at night and shake off the soot that floated down from the ceiling whenever the Spadina bus hissed to a stop out front. Only after passing that spectacle did the visitor encounter the office itself. The fact that such camouflage did nothing to diminish the traffic was all to the good, for to a remarkable degree Anansi depended on volunteer labourers, though for such a tiny company it offered a variety of employment options.

People with diverse backgrounds would soon go on to equally divergent futures. For example, the woman who designed the stylized spider that was Anansi's logo sold candy in one of the sleazy all-night cinemas on Yonge Street; I would sometimes see her there when I went to experience some camp Audie Murphy film at four in the morning. When asked why the spider she created had only six legs, she would always remark demurely, "The other two are up its ass." One of the sales people was an ex-soldier who lived above the Brunswick House tavern, another was a wavering divinity student, and there were poets in sullen profusion, so young and yet so misunderstood. The redoubtable Arden Cohen, the ex-wife of Matt Cohen, an early Anansi author, had found her way to Anansi because she was one of several U of T students (she was taking Chinese) who rented rooms in Dennis Lee's house. She started as production manager but soon became the conscience of the whole place and later, as Arden Ford, moved on to other trade houses and then to a career in scholarly publishing. Shirley Gibson appeared one day to put up posters for her husband Graeme Gibson's novel *Five Legs*, one of Dennis's epochal discoveries; she eventually wound up the president of the company.

There were usually one or two people from Dave's or Dennis's classes helping out as well. One of these lived in a commune on Brunswick Avenue that I soon began using as my other residence. This commune didn't have a religious or political underpinning; it existed merely to let a lot of people live inexpensively and make mischief. Among the communards there was, however, a freelance holy man named Kim, who had the authentic smell of the guru on him though I always suspected he came from the suburbs. For a time he was rather prominent in secret mystical circles.

"I keep hearing about his power," Dennis said one day. "Perhaps there's a book there."

"He can't write," I said. "I mean he doesn't. He's much too spiritual for that."

I once stayed up most of the night hunched in the corner of his bare room while he and a female co-suburbanist, who had not yet shed the outward manifestations of that lifestyle, worked their way through a truly extraordinary inventory of sexual positions, illuminated only by the candles on the floor and a transcendental inner glow.

Another resident was an ex-Nazi named Otto who lived there for economic reasons. He was a waiter by profession but his alcoholism kept pushing him to jobs in restaurants of less and less consequence. He told us once that he began to fear for his own life after a distant member of his family, a cousin if I remember correctly, was garrotted with piano wire after being implicated in the July 1944 attempt to assassinate Hitler. Drunk or sober, and he was usually the former, Otto never failed to polish his shoes each evening and align them with precision by his door. He aroused only pity rather than hatred or resentment, even from another resident who called himself the Rabbi for professional reasons. The Rabbi's profession was dope dealing.

Across the hall from the Rabbi lived an American deserter of immense charm who had escaped from a military prison and then a civilian one and had come north following a slow zig-zag course, working a few days at jobs that did not require sophisticated proof of his identity. The only such employment he could find in Chicago during Christmas 1966 was as a seasonal mail sorter in the federal building in the Loop. Each day an unsmiling special agent would descend from the FBI office upstairs to collect the mail. Each time he counted out the envelopes, wondering if one of them contained his own wanted poster. Now, in Toronto, he tried to support himself in various ways while studying criminology part-time. When the Drug Addiction Research Foundation began paying five dollars for true accounts of certain types of drug experiences, he approached those in charge with a proposition: three for twelve-fifty.

His girlfriend, a sweet, gentle person, much befuddled by the pressures of the day, had once tried to kill herself, leaving a note pleading self-defence. After she had undergone a long series of treatments, someone at 999 Queen, the provincial psychiatric hospital, issued her a document attesting to her sanity. It was intended to help in finding a job, but she would flash it whenever she experienced one of her devastating psychotic episodes. Once some of us had to restrain her. One person had grabbed her around the waist from behind and was trying to get her onto the bed, but she was flailing at us with her fists and waving this paper. "The government doesn't think I'm crazy," she screamed. Tears rolled down her cheeks. "*I have documentary proof!*" Forensically, of course, she did have the rest of us at a disadvantage.

Many's the night I left the basement cot at Anansi that severe winter and trudged through the deep snow to the Brunswick Avenue house, usually staying over, sleeping in my clothes in places ranging from some temporarily unoccupied sofa to the glassed-in summer porch, which was unheated. A couple of times I must have gained warmth through the rapidly shifting sexual alliances around that place. In 1983, when Katherine Govier published her short story collection *Fables of Brunswick Avenue*, I, and I imagine an unaccountably large number of other people our age, smiled in recollection at the name, though my fables, and theirs, may be different from the ones Katherine spins under that perfect piece of title-making.

Before coming to Toronto, I had had some correspondence and phone communication with Allen Ginsberg. I have a hazy memory of calling him about something on his birthday. I reached him at the home of his elderly father, Louis Ginsberg, in New Jersey. The senior Ginsberg was the traditional rhyming poet, a widower now, after many trying and destructive years with his sad psychotic wife, Naomi, as Allen described in *Kaddish* with such unforgettable power. In any case, I had got myself in the black phone book that Allen Ginsberg carried around, one of the most important practical documents of the sixties, for Allen would whip it out and put people in San Francisco in touch with ones in Tangier or Ahmadabad: it was a kind of secret bulletin board of the Movement, huge and highly efficient. So it was, somehow, that I knew he would be coming to Toronto to read at Hart House and that I was to be his handler.

My recollection of the immense Great Hall is that hippies and near-hippies took up every possible bit of space on the floor and along the wainscotting and may even have begun to hang from the mock-medieval beams, so to as make its benefactor, Vincent Massey, who had died only months earlier, perform at least one revolution in the family mausoleum.

Allen was the most compelling reader I had ever heard. Not a bombastic declaimer like Irving Layton, not a charmer and intensifier by turns, like Earle Birney. Certainly not the kind of defiant minimalist that Margaret Atwood, because of her platform monotone, sometimes appeared to be. He was funny and dirty, and he made punctuation with his fingers. The right forefinger and middle finger placed over his moustache and beard, with a space free for the mouth, was a sure sign of some impending emotional revelation, deeply felt and pried from the bottom of the consciousness only after years of other people's therapy and his own self-medicative techniques. The same position but accompanied with a gentle stroking of the beard while he talked was often the

signal for descriptive narrative—Allen at his most Whit-
manesque. Conversely, the forefinger suddenly raised
straight up in the air as though to illustrate a point was
always the signal for one of those Beat urban ironies of
his, the sentences delivered without much in the way of
definite or indefinite articles. They were a sign of hope
amid the chaos of the world. Chalk one up for the
human spirit, they said. At these, his voice would rise,
taking on a sweet tone, and his face assume a dear if not
downright beatific expression. With his finger-cymbals
and his little wooden harmonium, he wavered between
poetry and song, and took the listeners on a midway ride
of word-music, and rhythms and images—with the
word-music, I would say, always having the strongest
claim on the emotions, as music does. Later—I believe it
must have been at McMaster University, before an audience of, by comparison, rather straight university kids—
he sucked nerves and jacked off people's emotions all
night, performing those of his works most popular at
that moment. When he read his long anti-Vietnam War
poem "Wichita Vortex Sutra" and inserted the variant
lines "Language, language, there is no language left save
the ageless one of cocksuckers," the house broke down in
tears.

I had been trying to get moments here and there to
evangelize Allen about the work we were trying to do
with Anansi. I remember attempting this once when we
were rushing to a television taping in the back of a limo,
accompanied by a TV publicist named Lexy. Allen
interrupted, wanting to know what that black sky-
scraper was down by Lake Erie (unlike Whitman, he
always got Lakes Erie and Ontario confused, even in his

poetry). I told him it was the first phase of the T-D Centre. Toronto was early not late modernist in those days: no other big glass towers yet imposed themselves on the skyline. Now finally, after the Hart House reading, we were alone in one of the Massey College guest rooms by the porter's lodge, and he pumped me for more information. He also made a pass at me, but this was pro forma for Allen, and after being caught off guard just a second, I accepted the undeserved compliment with good humour, as there was no suggestion I was anybody special. After all, I knew this man's whole biography. How he had experienced a vision of Blake in the New York tenement in 1948. How he had been crowned Queen of the May in Czechoslovakia before being deported. How he had been similarly thrown out of Cuba, supposedly for saying that Fidel Castro's brother Raul was "cute" (an utterance that, if true, just goes to prove the old adage that one's man meat is, well, another man's meat). I knew that Allen would sometimes explain to people how Whitman had slept with one of his disciples, the poet and philosopher Edward Carpenter, who was supposed to have slept in turn with Gavin Arthur, an astrologer who was the grandson of President Chester A. Arthur. The younger Arthur is then said to have had an affair with Ellen Godfrey's friend Neal Cassady—whom Ginsberg, and of course Kerouac too, had been in and out of love with for years, requitedly so. Ergo, Allen would summarize, I have slept with Whitman.

Ginsberg's poetry as printed in books was almost always what he had taken from his notebooks, in which he scribbled more or less spontaneously as he ricochetted around the U.S. and the world in his role as alternative culture leader. Spontaneity was certainly the poetry's strength. The unrelieved nature of the spontaneity, however, was also its greatest defect, particularly when read on the page. In any case, he let me see his current poetry notebook at Massey that evening, and we copied out enough new poems to make a booklet for Anansi. This was typical of his dealings with various widely scattered small presses—anyone below the girth of City Lights, his primary imprint, presided over by his old friend Lawrence Ferlinghetti from above the City Lights bookshop in North Beach, San Francisco.

We talked much of the night. When I left, I walked the streets for a couple of hours and then had breakfast at a wonderful pure unreconstructed 1959 drugstore, the kind with magazine racks and a soda fountain, which stood on Hoskin Avenue (but not for too much longer—it was soon razed for the Robarts Library). Then I went back to 671 Spadina full of enthusiasm for the book that was about to be hatched. Allen had called the manuscript *Airplane Epiphanies*. Dennis later got him to change the title to *Airplane Dreams: Compositions from Journals*.

Simply being part of that address book of Allen's made one a member of an international secret order whose only obligations, as far as one could tell, were to put up (and put up with) those whom Allen sent your way. One afternoon a tall cadaverous fellow carrying a guitar case gave Ellen Godfrey a terrible start at the front door. She reported that he said, "Allen told me I could crash." She also picked up some additional message along the lines of "They're after me again." I apologized for the disturbance (I think she sighed) and hustled my charge downstairs. His name was Jerry Benjamin, though he wrote as "Jeremiah," and his guitar case turned out to hold, not a musical instrument, but most of his worldly effects—poetry and play manuscripts, which others had not found very publishable, and one great prize indeed, a dramatized version of Ginsberg's *Kaddish*, which Allen had given him permission to have produced in Toronto if possible. This was typical of Allen, who was as generous with his work and reputation as with his money, which he was forever giving away to other poets.

During the Beat ascendancy, I learned, Benjamin had been a considerable figure in certain theatrical circles in New York. He directed the first productions of *Arise, Arise* by Louis Zukofsky and *Ankle Sox and Jive Shoelaces* by John Weiners, as well as those of a pair of plays, *The Baptism* and *The Toilet*, by LeRoi Jones (later Imamu Amiri Baraka). His role in these last two events was duly acknowledged in the playscripts published by Grove Press. Some other amazing old evidence of his glory would also surface from the wodge of papers in his guitar case (a gift from Allen, he said). One was a decaying *New York Times* clipping from 1959 showing a photograph of two avant-garde filmmakers at work, Andy Warhol and Jerry Benjamin, both of whom were virtually unknown at the time. Jeremiah would always remain so. He looked much different now than in the yellowing half-tone, because at some subsequent point he had had his teeth extracted.

Dave was uneasy having this character crashing, however briefly, in his basement and so threw him out or rather ordered me to do it. Jeremiah took it quite well, as I got him on one of those days when he projected the artificial gentleness then associated with acid heads. After that he would come and go, never staying long in the city but never long out of it either. I think of him as one of the hundreds of bizarre characters attracted to the place in those days when chaos reigned only a short distance to the south. The situation, I imagine, must have been very similar to the one that obtained in Toronto and Montreal during the American Civil War a hundred years earlier, when, as contemporary accounts suggest, Canada was full of exiles and spies—that is, those who cared too much and were sad and those who cared too little and were angry.

I think Benjamin must have been in Buffalo when he wasn't hanging around Anansi and the other stops on his Toronto rounds, for he seems to have had links to some of the writers there, such as a wild former merchant seaman who wrote long poems about Che Guevera, or maybe even to Allen De Loach, the poetry czar of Buffalo. In any case, one night I was walking in Chinatown and ran into him carrying his guitar case, and he told me he had just got into town at the bus station at Bay and Edward. We began to talk and stroll, stroll and talk, heading generally in a westerly direction towards a vast area of undifferentiated streets where immigrant women sometimes let rooms. Now in those days, a diligent transient might—just might—find a room for ten dollars a week. I watched with amazement as Benjamin, using some mysterious primal sense or instinct, located without direct enquiry of any kind, what was surely Toronto's or North America's only *five-dollar* room. It was just big enough to allow one chair and a bed, and the chair had to be moved out of the way when one opened the door.

He paid the landlady two weeks' rent and when she left started to unpack his guitar case and change his clothes. He was wearing bellbottoms and a bright floral shirt that hung loosely on his skinny frame.

"Allen's always telling me to do what he does and buy durable cheap clothes in the Army and Navy," he said. He gave a look to indicate that he had tried but was a natural-born slave to fashion, what he could he do?

When he took off his pants, I saw that he had a belt of marijuana wrapped around his waist. He removed it carefully and tucked it under the pillow.

I was amazed. "Aren't you afraid to cross the border like that?"

"Not at all. In the theatre you learn how to make yourself the master of other people's impressions of you."

On a certain crude level, he was right. I remember once standing with Dennis at the traffic roundabout at St. George and Hoskin when Benjamin came up behind us and we went somewhere for coffee. Dennis was always unkind about Benjamin's writing (it was indeed drivel) but never to his face, and by comparison to Dave at least, was always somewhat partial to him, though perhaps reluctantly. Dennis asked him what progress he was making on the *Kaddish* project.

"I have begun the first round of auditions," Benjamin replied. "So many attractive young people. I encourage them all to disrobe completely. I find it creates a good working atmosphere."

Dennis said nothing but looked surprised. Benjamin explained that, well, some people get upset and leave and those are the ones without a future in the theatre.

Like so many figures of the time, Jerry Benjamin simply disappeared one day, creating an absence that would be noticed only in long nostalgic retrospect. I last heard of him in the late 1970s when the catalogue of an American antiquarian bookseller listed some relatively recent poetry chapbook of his. I remember that it had a California imprint. That must be where he went. Years later, in 1981, there was, finally, a Toronto production of a play based on *Kaddish*, but not one that Jerry Benjamin had anything to do with as far as research can reveal. He would be in his sixties now, I guess.

———————

In the 1970s, after they had forced the provincial government to stop the Spadina Expressway, which would have cut across the heart of the city, destroying the whole by ruining the constituent neighbourhoods, everybody in Toronto aspired to be some kind of urban affairs expert. Unsupervised gangs of self-taught city planners and land-use critics were permitted to roam the streets freely, writing essays and being aggressively earnest. Later, many of them actually took over the municipal government from the property developers and other rogues who traditionally controlled it. This gave Toronto, if not a *belle époque*, then a little civic respite, such as it enjoyed once before—in the 1890s when a reform movement overthrew what one historian calls the "usual band of thieves and horse traders who occupied City Hall." But in the late 1960s nobody in Toronto yet wanted to be an urbanist. In those days the people I was acquainted with all wished to be educational reformers.

Personally, I found it hard to be more than just generally sympathetic with their views. I had concluded that education, which I wanted badly, was one of those things that if one wished done right one had better do oneself. That was the very essence of what I saw myself becoming in the world: a kind of radical whig autodidact. To reject the Tory idea that one was given a job description at birth was essential to also rejecting the idea that one was signed up at birth for a particular ideology, as though it was an exclusive private school with a waiting list a generation long. I wanted to educate myself, make myself into a humane person. I also wanted to show that anti-Americanism could be a grid for responding to the world, that one could at least privately use it as a full-blown economic, moral and philosophical *ism*, as Marxism or Christianity were or feminism would soon become. Of America, I thought, one could spend one's existence trying to attain, in an almost Buddhist way, an ever higher and more perfect form of rejection. I couldn't truly connect with these nice kids who were excitedly reading Jerry Farber's much-reprinted essay "The Student As Nigger" and demonstrating because their classes at the University of Toronto were too crowded. Their destructive energy had originated on campuses below the border, so I could applaud when at least part of what they did here had the effect of returning the missiles on a long arc.

But I couldn't muster anything like empathy. The campus, where I often had cause to go, selling Anansi titles into the U of T Book Room on the quad, gave me a chilly feeling that found expression in a haiku I wrote years later:

Art flourishes in strange precincts
life drawing offered at the morgue
books written at the university.

But Dennis was of another view completely. As first a student and then a teacher there, he had come to rail against the impersonal not to say dehumanizing nature of a place as large and bureaucratic as the U of T. The composition of the institution was such that it seemed to him to render the mission—the infusing of liberal education—impossible. With many others, such as a John Stuart Mill scholar and frequent Anansi contributor named John Robson (who lived around the corner from the press), he came to speak and write of the horrors of the multiversity (a California coinage). In fact, he was coming to fundamentally rethink the process of education at all levels. This led, ultimately and improbably, to the erection of an eighteen-storey high-rise at Bloor and Huron, a block from Anansi. It was called Rochdale College, and was by far the biggest drug supermarket that Canada and maybe the eastern half of North America had ever seen. More importantly, it was a closed dystopian society of the most rigid kind, an authoritarian nightmare of a place where biker gangs, hired as security forces, set up checkpoints in the lobby and patrolled the corridors with vicious dogs: precisely the opposite of what poor Dennis had envisioned.

The story is this. Dennis was one of those rare people whose love of education couldn't be separated from his genuine love of children, his own and other people's (a quality made public later when he stumbled into a remarkably lucrative career as a writer of verse for kids). Just as repulsion with the multiversity was a reaction that he and the others frankly admitted they had taken from conditions at Berkeley, so Rochdale was tied in with Everdale, an alternative free school some people in Toronto were running, modelled on A.E. Neill's Summerhill in England. The Everdale group integrated crafts and unstructured tutoring. They even had a printing press. Dennis's *Kingdom of Absence* had been printed on it (before Dave put Anansi on a more businesslike footing, with the year's list contracted out to a large commercial printing house paid for by a line of credit at a bank in faraway Mississauaga, where Dave, after some diligent searching, had located that rarest of all creatures, a branch manager who liked publishing). The Everdale people published a stubby, self-involved journal of their ideas called *This Magazine Is about Schools* (which, under different guidance, evolved in time into *This Magazine*, the periodical of general political comment). It had offices in one of the Huron Street houses of Campus Co-op, the well-established organization that fixed up big old places all round the edge of the campus as a means of providing decent student accommodation at low cost.

Campus Co-op had long been as modest as its aims, but recently it had taken off, expanding in all directions.

This frenzy of non-profit enterprise was instigated by Howard Adelman, a contemporary of Dennis's, now teaching philosophy at York University. The two of them, but with Dennis, I think, the theorist of the pair, founded Rochdale as a college within the university where students would live and work independently of the normal university structure, running the place by purely democratic means, forming into seminars as organic need suggested, breaking away for solitary work when that appeared the better course instead: no faculty, no grades, none of the oppressive infrastructure of the old way: what Dennis would call "Rochdale's doctrinaire unwillingness to prescribe or proscribe any activity whatever as educational for the person carrying it on." The quotation is from his essay "Getting to Rochdale," a confession of his disillusionment with the university and of his search for alternatives. It was a piece that exerted a tremendous pull on people's thought at the time but would soon come to seem rather innocent.

In the essay he went on to knock off several possible criticisms of what he was doing. "The issue which Rochdale raised was this: were we not recreating a more libertarian version of [the liberal education of old] with our attempt to allow people to do what they pleased? If I can write poems and you can write poems and John Jordan can read Greek, and nobody will ever say us nay, are we not going even further toward making a specious virtue out of our own poverty in the face of that root question, 'What is it good to know?'" What caught my eye was the use of *libertarian*. As far as I know, Dennis was not familiar with, or even much interested in, the vast literature on intentional communities nor with any sort of anarchist theory of decentralization except as it applied *ad hoc* in this one particular situation. Maybe this is what made the experiment so interesting. Maybe this is what made it such a disaster.

Adelman I never knew well, but looking back now I can't help but wonder whether he was another Dave Godfrey in Dennis's life: another scholar-entrepreneur who made Dennis feel inadequate at being only, supremely, the thing before the hyphen and not, by skill or temperament, the thing that followed it. Anyway, with Adelman turned a kind of anti-development developer, in command of the fund-raising, Rochdale moved from the six Co-op houses to the high-rise, financed with a mortgage from the federal government. I would chart the progress as I walked along Bloor every day, and remember the moment when the cranes and the hoardings came down and the finishing work began. The essential and immutable problem, of course, is that Rochdale was to be two things to two sets of people: an immensely valuable piece of co-op real estate to some, a laboratory for further educational experiments to others. The educationalists thought it great that their people should study and live in the same space, which they would administer themselves in totally egalitarian fashion, but that convenient dual function was hardly essential to their idea of what they meant by *community*. For their part, the real-estate types didn't need the educators or particularly care about them.

Dennis was to be one of two "resource persons" at Rochdale when the new temple to unstructured education was complete. In his essay he tells of first being concerned with the size and location of their offices there, when someone from the crowd of rabble asked who he imagined he was to think in those terms. His first response was defensiveness, "because I thought somebody was sniping at me. After a bit, though, we realized that he was perfectly right. Why should two members of the college have offices to themselves when we are crying for space? And, more important, wouldn't that institutionalize everything we were trying to get beyond both in other people's responses and in ourselves?" This reminds me of an essay by that equally good and great soul, Paul Goodman, about the proper democratic way for people to arrange the chairs when meeting in solemn session to change the world. We think of the 1960s as a time when bureaucracy was suppressed for a while. In fact, it merely assumed an alias.

Dennis said that he often recalled the scriptural passage in which Christ advises the lads to be as crafty as serpents and as innocent as doves. Dear Dennis was always a model of dove-like behaviour but in this instance fell sadly short in the snake department. Once the Rochdale high-rise was completed (amid dark rumours about who might have benefited from its construction), everything utopian about it started to come to a halt. It did attract some important developments in art (all of them collective or corporate, not individual), as when General Idea and Theatre Passe Muraille were hatched or for that matter when Stan Bevington relocated Coach House Press to another coach house, almost identical to the one on Bathurst Street, in an alley to the rear. But these developments also had to do with the cheap rent and availability of sex and other necessities of life as they were then understood. What the place was most famous for, and justly, was its violence and drugs and disorder.

Right from the start Rochdale was a media circus, as reporters tried to respond to every fresh rumour of some LSD-induced suicide from the roof or a drug-related murder. Three levels of police were constantly trying to infiltrate the place when not actually raiding it, partly no doubt because of the way Rochdale became a magnet for thrill-seekers from all over the continent and even Europe. What happened at Haight-Ashbury in San Francisco in 1967 on a broad horizontal plane was repeated at Rochdale in Toronto the following year, and the year after that and the year after that, in a tall vertical space that could be made fairly secure against unwanted intrusion. This only increased the paranoia of the authorities without, which in turn did the same for the paranoia of those within. It became the most Americanized place in Toronto, not excluding the U.S. Consulate on University Avenue: a kind of tower of urban decay and social chaos, reaching to the sky above the Annex. At one point, Rochdale was home to a group of satanists that exerted an influence on the thinking of Charles Manson, according to the Manson book by Ed Sanders, my old Fug-leader.

I never contradict the people I meet these days who reminisce warmly of the time they lived at Rochdale (where some of them purchased the phoney college degrees the Rochdalers were always peddling—the ultimate insult to Dennis, I suppose). They were usually away from home for the first time and speak now with easy nostalgia, surrounded by the middle-class comforts to which they've long since returned. For myself, at the time, I couldn't always avoid Rochdale. To be sure, I had a few friends there. A likeable Dutch fellow named Bernie Bomers was the Rochdale business manager (a title full of pyrotechnic irony); later he was a teller at the Bank of Nova Scotia across from the Victory Burlesk on Spadina, where he got to know all the strippers as they came to cash their cheques; he and I and two young women from Saskatoon once drove frantically, non-stop, to Quebec City, on a sort of urgent mission of joy whose meaning escapes me completely now. But Rochdale struck me as a place to bypass when possible. Too much armed posturing, too much publicity. Certainly there was nobody there learning anything, as far as I could tell, even studying anything, or even reading much.

When it all started to turn sour so poisonously, which was almost at once, Dennis resigned, and the other idealists were soon given the sack. I think Rochdale must have been a great pain in Dennis's heart for years afterwards. I bring up the subject here because it also had a profound effect on Anansi.

One of Dave Godfrey's causes was finding a cheap means of feeding the hungry in Africa. To this end he had invented a product called Makka. The name, he said, was composed of syllables that were common to all the world's languages. Makka was a powdered substance which when mixed with water was supposed to provide one adult with a drink containing all the nutrients and vitamins necessary for a single day's healthy existence. It came in foil pouches and tasted terrible, just terrible. For though Makka never got into production, there were many cartons of the prototype batch lying round the Anansi office, and I had to dip into them from time to time to supplement my own Third World diet.

Another of Dave's causes, at least briefly, was SUPA, the Student Union for Peace Action, which Dennis was involved with for a while too. SUPA occupied a little green building at 658 Spadina which over the years, until finally razed in the 1980s, would house a startling succession of political groups, not excluding the Trotskyites. One of SUPA's many projects, started as early as 1965, was helping American draft resisters settle in Canada as a means of avoiding or protesting the Vietnam War. They published a pamphlet entitled *Escape from Freedom* (I always wondered whether the title was supposed to echo Erich Fromm). As the SUPA initiative led eventually to the much more professional body called the Toronto Anti-Draft Programme, so did the pamphlet lead to a book, notorious and helpful in its day, the *Manual for Draft-Age Immigrants to Canada*, which, through Dave's brokerage, was published jointly by the TADP and Anansi. Both the *Manual* and *The University Game*, the essay collection edited by Howard Adelman and Dennis and containing "Getting to Rochdale," appeared in January 1968. They were both runaway successes, garnering an enormous amount of attention, most of it positive, and going quickly into second and third printings. At this remove, they seem to me to represent the dimorphic and perhaps therefore unworkable nature of Anansi as it was at that stage.

The *Manual* was a product of Dave's entrepreneurial social activism, so ahead of its time. The title-page
bore the name of Mark Satin, the publicity-conscious
head of TADP (who I once heard say, "Anonymity
would kill me"); he later moved back home and was
among the first to popularize the term New Age. In
fact, though, the *Manual* was a packaged sort of book,
rather than one that had been written or even edited (in
the sense that an anthology would be). It was clever,
being designed to look as much as possible like a Government of Canada publication you would find at the
Queen's Printer on Yonge Street. And it was controversial. Anansi immediately became the object of government surveillance. A couple of years later, a Bell Canada
lineman doing some routine work took aside a friend of
mine who was staying at the old Anansi place and
showed him how clumsily the Mounties or the Metro
Police intelligence unit had tapped the phones. "Look
at this," the repairman said in resignation and disgust,
pointing to some crude wiring. "They're always using
this crap." The fact that Dave very soon afterwards did
an about-face on the whole question of U.S. draft
evaders, seeing them as agents of the great contamina-
tion, doesn't detract from my picture of the book as a
perfect expression of his genius. Rather, it enhances it.

Like so many other Canadian couples, Dennis and
Donna Lee were counselling draft dodgers one evening
a week. They would form little groups in their living
room up at the other end of Brunswick Avenue, close to
Dupont. They too became disillusioned with what they
were doing. But their gradual turning away was not the
same as Dave's abrupt rejection, any more than *The*

University Game, with its earnest dove-like mission of enquiry, resembled Dave's *Manual*, which seemed to seek useful subversion in the marriage of politics and commerce. Compared to Dennis and most other people, Dave was always extreme in his politics, which meant that he was more prone to swings as well. Dennis was a standard liberal humanist and poet who just chanced, by some genetic happenstance, to be brilliant. Which is not the same thing as being worldly—the commoner quality by a factor of millions, but also one, it seemed to me, Dennis sometimes appeared to know he lacked. Dennis was one of those writers, far more numerous now than then, who struggled anxiously to write seriously without disdaining or rejecting the popular culture. For me, the best illustration was the libretto he wrote for a John Beckwith cantata about Toronto. Dennis worked in the street cries of the news butchers selling the *Star* and the *Telegram*. So now, striving to do something about Dave's implicit put-downs, he drew his politics more and more from the civic side of his general nature, where the pop cult stuff resided with his strange personal mix of art and Christianity.

No coincidence, then, that his next Anansi publication was *Civil Elegies*. I speak of the first edition, a simply designed, squarish book in blue and grey wrappers. It is textually much different from the edition of 1972 and also much more difficult to locate in decent condition, as most of the run was ruined by water damage after being stored in what was originally the coal bin of the Anansi house. The book came out in April 1968, at just about the time that I was upstairs one evening talking to Dave about the day's book

orders when Ellen flew in the front door in an agitated
state to say that Martin Luther King had been killed.
We wouldn't know it for a long time, but the assassin,
James Earl Ray, had slipped out of the U.S. and into
Toronto, with the help of accomplices in whom the
authorities would never take much interest. He would
soon be hanging around the Silver Dollar Room, a
tavern just down Spadina, at College, past the Cres-
cent.

That was an astonishing year, an *annus mirabilis*,
one of those watershed times that just pop up in history
every now and then, like 1848 or 1939. For those of us
wrapped up in the unfolding horror of the war, it was
the year of the Tet Offensive, which began at the end of
January. In a coordinated series of surprises, the Vietcong and North Vietnamese regulars swept into
Danang and other seaports where the Americans had
important bases. They captured a hundred cities and
towns in the Delta and made similar inroads in the
highlands and up in the mountains. In Saigon, which
was not only the capital but America's impregnable
jukebox hometown-in-exile, VC attacked the airport,
the radio station and the presidential palace. In a particularly lovely bit of symbolism, they blasted their way
inside the U.S. Embassy compound—then left. Within
a few months they'd let the Americans reclaim it all, to
remind them just how overextended the empire had
become. In later years U.S. revisionists, writing for
those coming along afterwards, would pooh-pooh the
importance of the Tet. But anybody looking at the
events at the time could see clearly enough what had
happened. General Giap had served notice that though

the Vietnamese were weak in everything but stamina they would still win, by chasing the woolly mammoth until it dropped. It took another seven years for the Americans, so very much stronger than their enemy yet so badly out-soldiered, to pack up. Seven years seem scarcely to have made a dent in Vietnamese resolve.

Dave and Dennis were having open spats now as their two personalities, and two visions of publishing and life and Canada, came into conflict. I can remember Dave sweeping in one morning and saying offhandedly to everyone who happened to be there, "Don't be alarmed, but it looks like we may have to publish a book by John Robert Colombo." Dennis could see he wasn't kidding, that Dave must have committed to some scheme as a trade-off against part of some other scheme, neither of which he (Dennis) knew anything about. He looked wounded and perturbed. (The book, whatever it was, never materialized.) On another occasion, Dave said to me, "You'd think somebody with the brains to get a Ph.D. could figure out how to run a small business." In fact, Dennis, unlike Dave, didn't have his doctorate, but that was beside the point. At one stage I saw some books on elementary finance and commercial practice lying on Dennis's desk. Faced with a problem, he must have been doing what I always do: seek out the phrase books and grammars and see how to teach myself enough to get out of trouble. Dave, I imagine, found such a response risible. In May, with the spring term at Trinity over, Dave and his family decamped for France, where he would write his long-awaited African novel, *The New Ancestors*.

None of the parties involved could have foreseen

this, but the Godfreys' departure brought me a great gift which has enriched me down through the years. Dave sublet the house to a young couple, Daniel and Judy Williman and their three small daughters. Dan was a politically active expat American but not a draft resister. He had once been immune from service as a Catholic seminarian; later, his records were among those destroyed by the famous renegade priests, Ted and Daniel Berrigan, in their raid on the draft board at Catonsville, Maryland. He was teaching a course at York (commuting there by bicycle because he was so poor) while doing advanced study at the Pontifical Institute of Mediaeval Studies. He was a fourteenth-century man, moving towards his licentiate or Vatican Ph.D., with a huge multi-volume work on the manuscripts collected by the Avignon popes through the papal right of spoil. This effort would go on for years, in time, I believe, becoming one of the first original applications of computer technology to medieval studies. This was characteristic of Dan, who soon became a close friend. He had great technical and mechanical gifts which reminded me of my father's. As a matter of course, he made the family furniture and taught himself trades as complicated as printing. Later, when they had a couple of acres of space, he grew their food, including wheat, which he'd flail by hand. I'm proud to say that I once helped him (not very successfully, it's true, as I inherited none of Father's manual skill) with a house he was building on the Bruce Peninsula, for he was a decent self-taught architect as well.

Another trait I liked in Dan was that he saw teaching and learning as inseparable functions. He knew so much—in history, in law, in research disciplines like paleography—that I couldn't help but learn from him, though he never slipped into a pedagogic diction; giving and taking knowledge, it was all part of a natural flow. He knew the importance of ceremony—he was, like me, a person in search of a continuum to climb aboard—but strove to live simply and enjoy his fellow creatures and their best handiwork. He read voraciously in all fields, all areas, listened to all the music old and new, looked at all art and cinema, searching for the highest quality goods so that he could offer himself totally on the altar of complete soul-cleansing enjoyment. He and Judy practised charity as well. I remember how, the first time they received a windfall—an academic prize or a tiny inheritance, I can't remember which—they promptly sent cheques to all the people they knew who were less materially well off than they were. That was typical of them. Judy, for instance, was convinced I was heading for a physical collapse, sleeping in the cold basement, living on caffeine and goddam Makka, and never warmly enough dressed, so she seconded me for their family breakfasts each morning.

Dan threw himself into the life and culture of whatever community he was in (a quality I always find easy to admire as I recognize it in myself), but he was also that rarest of birds, the totally cosmopolitan American, relaxed and authentic in his moveable comforts. He could go almost anywhere in the English-speaking world at almost any level of society with only the most minor vowel adjustments. He moved pretty freely among the French and the Italians also (and when I first got to know him was successfully teaching himself German from the cheapest titles available at a little German bookshop down Spadina). Like the rest of us, he had his blockages and inherited obstacles to freedom. In his case they came from a strong father, an acquiescent mother, and the all-powerful culture of the Catholic Church, whose shadow was getting shorter but blacker the whole time he was growing up. We've followed each other through years of *problemas sentimentales* as well as *problemas economicos*. In one of his letters I find him speaking of his "divorce car" with the explanation: "The Latin *divortium* primarily signifies the branching of a road, while *repudium* was used to mean the dissolution of a marriage contract; once again, an aging culture returns to verify the poetry of an earlier age, as the typical marriage dissolution now requires the purchase of a separate vehicle."

I've learned a lot (but not as much as I wish I could learn) from his example. About, for instance, seeking the perfect Tolstoyean balance of mind work and body work, of being respectful of the past as a tool of the present, of going at each new day like a rescued castaway tasting ice cream again for the first time.

———

As I've said, Anansi had at least collateral connections to both Rochdale and the anti-war movement. Of these I was more interested in the latter, which in fact came to touch me directly.

Fed by images in movies, younger people now believe that it was the U.S. military itself that was selecting who would be drafted and who not. Such a national scheme under direct military control would have carried its own problems with it, but by its very bureaucratic facelessness it would have been fairer than the one that was actually in place. The Selective Service Act empowered local committees in each large and small community to do the necessary selecting and rejecting, according to various quotas. To keep paperwork from going astray as it flew back and forth across the country, one's fate was always determined by the district one resided in the instant one turned eighteen. An eighteen-year-old living in Boston or Greenwich Village could thus pretty much be assured of liberal treatment, an eighteen-year-old in some hotbed of illiberalism (why single out one or two from the thousands available for naming?) was likely to "serve." These local boards might be made up of a used-car dealer, an undertaker, a lawyer, a football coach, all of them political appointees with the power of life and death. In addition to making regional inequities inevitable, they also made worse the class and racial biases already built into the national guidelines for exceptions and deferments based on educational status.

Of the many hundreds of thousands who protested by doing more than simply staying on in college or university, the biggest category, it seems to me, were those primarily protesting the unfairness of the draft, as I think it was perfectly legitimate and necessary to do. Next came a smaller but more solid group who were earnestly protesting the war and were often committed pacifists. Finally there was a third category, which didn't preclude membership in the other two: those such as myself (I met very few others) who simply didn't want to be Americans any more ever again and would spend the rest of their lives trying to deal with the moral guilt of having had the misfortune to be born in the United States. I've never found *draft dodger* a useful term unless used precisely. The draft dodgers were of two types: the ones who stopped coming to Canada after the Selective Service introduced a lottery system which at least gave non-fighters a fighting chance, and the ones who, if they were in Canada before the lottery, went back home after the limited amnesty of President Gerald Ford or the universal one of his successor, Jimmy Carter. Of course, many who might have returned if still young and single, chose to remain because they had started careers or families that they couldn't or wouldn't uproot.

My own situation was typically surreal. When I duly registered, shortly before leaving the country, I was routinely classed I-A, ready for shipment to the paddies. I said: No, no, there's been a mistake. While my brother is in the navy, I'm contributing to the support of my widowed mother whose condition (they assumed physical, based on some misleading evidence; I meant mental) left her unfit for work. I was reclassified IV-A, a hardship case. I never got called up for physical, psychological or patriotic tests, none of which I would have passed if the game wasn't rigged too badly. Even with the dealer using marked cards, I couldn't have passed them all. Believe it or not, stuttering was one of the disqualifying handicaps; I had a therapeutic history going back to 1955 and on a bad day couldn't utter a complete sentence. And my patriotic health was even then a matter of public concern, FBI file and all. Personally, I thought I deserved, as a reward for long residence on the edge, the coveted I-Y, or psychiatric deferment. In any case, memory tells me that when I settled in Canada I even gave the board my change of address, as the law required. Whereupon the local burghers in Wheeling decided to draft me on the basis of the post-mark. They kept sending me orders to report to various places for induction, which I naturally threw in the rub-bish with an oath appropriate to each.

Down by King and Bathurst in those days there was a storefront bookshop, almost never open, filled with books from Dick Higgins's Something Else Press in New York and Ferlinghetti's City Lights Books in San Francisco, two lines for which the proprietor of the shop, a strange individual named Harry Fine, had somehow obtained Canadian distribution rights. Harry was a recovering businessman—an accountant, I believe—who had, as people said in those days, turned on, tuned in and dropped out. Sort of. Eventually he would devote himself totally to consciousness expan-sion and related pursuits. At the moment, though, he was in an uncertain middle stage between Bay Street and Nirvana, analogous, I suppose, to the awkward position in which a pre-op transsexual finds him/her-self. The way one knew of Harry's predicament was that he still wore his expensive three-piece suits but with a turban at one end and what looked like Vietcong san-dals at the other.

He lived on the second floor, above the seldom-opened bookshop, where he supposedly published an underground newspaper and certain works of erotica.

Leaks in the ceiling dripped brown water onto the new electric typewriters and expensive typesetting equipment. For staff, he had a few hangers-on, one of them a bear-like biker dressed in khaki (you could still read his rank and outfit in the silhouettes of thread where the flashes had been sewn on). He was stoned all the time—on what, I'm not sure—and he kept saluting people, as a kind of involuntary action. Whenever he saluted in his perpetually goofed-up state, he would giggle. There's something mildly stressogenic about a 240-pound biker giggling. Another of the people who hung about Fine's shop and, who knows?, may even have been paid for his obvious work, was James Ellis. This acquaintance of mine was a pioneer in Vietnam draft evasion, having come to Canada in late 1964. The notorious dungeon at Marion, Illinois, had not yet opened in 1964, and Alcatraz, which had been built originally to house two categories of prisoners—A) those too spirited for the rest of the federal prison system, and B) pacifists—had only recently been shut down. But the authorities still took a stern view of what they judged Jim to be guilty of. Although there was a twenty-year statute of limitations on draft offences, it didn't include any time spent outside the U.S., and the sentence if you were caught on their side of the border could be five years in federal prison. The danger had been brought home forcefully once, a couple of years before I met him, when Jim was flying on the newly named Air Canada from Vancouver to Toronto to get married. Because of severe snow storms, the pilot announced he was putting down in Cleveland. Jim thought of cutting up his ID and ditching it in the toilet. He thought of trying to switch ID with someone else. He even thought of refusing to deplane and seeing what the law said about an Air Canada plane providing legal or at least moral sanctuary. Instead, after a panicky half-hour or so, he decided to bluff his way through, which worked fine. He was lucky.

Now the marriage had collapsed and, growing weary of the pharmaceutically induced gridlock on King Street, Jim decided to return to Vancouver. On the third and topmost floor of King Street lived a sexual philanthropist named Ruth, who during much of this whole period was sharing her place with a five-member rock band of some local acclaim. The band was breaking up, regrouping, mutating, metamorphosing, as rock groups were forever doing, and Jim was able to acquire their VW van, which was covered, front, top, sides and back, with carefully revised graffiti, in which the band members took the same pride a Regency dandy would have taken in his epigrams. In lieu of his unpaid wages from Harry Fine, which were undeniably long in arrears and nowhere in sight, Jim appropriated the stock of City Lights books, which filled the back of the van, and so, in that condition, set off. He was sending cards urging me to join him and open a bookshop in Kitsilano.

Growing up in the atmosphere I did left me a dread of ultimatums and most other types of personal confrontation. To this day I can't bear television programmes on which people talk too loud. By now the undercurrent of hostility at Anansi was growing more powerful, and I begged an unpaid vacation to hitchhike west. Jim, when I found him, was living in a chaotic environment in one of those old frame houses with the wide porches (nearly every one of them gone now) that used to be the standard domestic architecture in much of the West End. The place was decorated mostly with Moroccan chimes and a few sticks of broken furniture which others had intended for the dump. He had traded or sold the books for food, and the famous van had somehow become a matched set of 1953 Austins, acquired from someone who was going to prison. He kindly gave me one for my trouble, but one day when I wasn't paying attention, I forgot to notice where I'd parked it. No doubt it was impounded by the police eventually. I had no intention of enquiring.

In those days, when the health department was more relaxed in such matters, there were three rather famous hole-in-the-wall restaurants in an unmarked Chinatown alley between Pender and Hastings. They had no names so far as English-speakers could determine but were known by the colours of their doors—Green, Orange, and Red, I think—and were always spoken of collectively as the Doors. Each was one small square room, half below the level of the laneway. At two of them you could get a bowl of steamed rice for five cents, and at one of the three, I forget which, a respectable enough portion of barbecued pork for a quarter. Thus you could keep yourself going for a base rate of only thirty cents per diem. The police were troublesome in Vancouver in those days, but the city was, then and forever, crawling with writers, and the livin' was generally easy. Not for the last time in my life, I made the mistake of not staying there permanently.

When I got back to Anansi, there was a business card of an RCMP officer in my pigeonhole with a note that I call him immediately. The message was weeks old. I phoned and went to meet him above the post office on St. Clair Avenue East. He informed me that the FBI had enquired after my whereabouts and happiness and asked what my intentions were. He then pulled the oldest trick in the book, I couldn't believe it. He produced a fat manila file labelled FETHERLING, put it on top of his desk, then excused himself for a few moments to attend to some other matter in another room. I didn't bite. He returned and we parted cordially, he in the knowledge that I was staying where I was, I with a fresh understanding that matters were picking up speed in Wheeling.

What was happening there, it turned out, was that I was indicted *in absentia* and a bench warrant was sworn out for me as a fugitive. A deputy United States marshall went to my mother's house in a vain attempt to serve me with it and instead ended up becoming Mother's boyfriend. He was very near retirement even then. He came from a town called Cameron, one county distant, and from a family that had made a little money in the Sistersville oil boom of the 1920s. As he had no relatives left, save one nephew, the money stuck to him. He was a stern, authoritarian man who, paradoxically, looked the image of Henry Miller. Mother would sometimes telephone me to report gleefully that through his influence she was going to work for the FBI. This was an assertion that not even the low regard in which I held my loyal antagonist J. Edgar Hoover could make me believe. A shameful admission, but she wasn't smart enough to work for the FBI, or almost anyone else, and indeed had held no regular employment

since 1938. What she was doing, I eventually learned
when I subpoenaed some of my files years later, was
simply volunteering information about me to the draft
authorities. Mother being Mother, she got almost all of
it wrong.

She called this new man of hers Mac, and once he
hung up his side arm and handcuffs, they spent almost
every evening together for the next twenty years, drinking and playing bingo. Mother treated him horribly
behind his back and sometimes not much better to his
face, but he was as pathetically lonely as she was, and he
suffered more and more as time went on from an
astounding list of serious illnesses and diseases, including emphysema so severe he could walk only a few yards
at a time. Mother was determined she was going to out-
live him and get the money. The race was going to be a
close one. By the end of the 1980s she had recovered
from one operation for bowel cancer and was ambulatory while his emphysema worsened and he became
permanently bedfast. The finish appeared to be in sight
but no one could call it. Her cancer showed signs of a
recurrence, though this was matched by Mac's heart,
which was deteriorating rapidly.

One night she telephoned me out of the blue to
inform me that I was a disgrace to her, to her family, to
my dead father's memory, to the United States and to
the entire white race. I could feel only varying degrees
of contempt for the rest of her list, but her inclusion of
number three hurt me deeply. She ended by slamming
down the receiver, as usual. A few months later, while
watching the television she could never quite understand, she dropped dead of a heart attack, her first,

which no one had been expecting. She was seventy-eight. Mac died not long afterwards. The nephew got the money.

There was an enormous party at Anansi; I believe the only publishing party Anansi ever threw in that wonderful old house on Spadina. My memory places the event in the late summer of 1969. From cellar to garret, the place was jammed with people, elbow to elbow. As far as the outside world knew, the press was in its glory. In remarkably short order it had put together a small backlist that contained a few titles, *The Circle Game* for instance, that would go on selling forever. At the same time, it was pushing ahead with all sorts of innovations. Until this point, Anansi had been known more for its poetry than for its fiction, but this was about to change, signalling, I think, the rise of a whole generation who would monopolize attention for years to come, including the novelists who a few years later would be instrumental in setting up the Writers' Union.

Dennis was now getting more interested in finding the young fiction writers (fiction was Dave's old turf), and he conceived a series of short, cheaply produced works called Spiderline Editions. They were uniform in their simplicity and their role in launching careers. Matt Cohen's first book was a Spiderline, *Korsoniloff*, which began a steady production of ever more sophisticated books to come from him in the decades ahead. Another first book was the Spiderline *Fallout* by Peter Such, a figure who would be quite important through the 1970s as a novelist with an interest in aboriginal peoples, archaeology, Canadian composers: an interesting fellow. Like some Anansi initiatives of a later era—for example, the Lost Works series edited by Margaret Atwood—the Spiderline idea was shortlived, with only five books in all. The others were *Eating Out* by John Sandman, *The Telephone Pole* by Russell Marois, and *A Perte de Temps* by Pierre Gravel.

Marois, a Quebecois who wrote in English, I got to know better than the others because, having no other place to work on *The Telephone Pole*, he would come into the Anansi basement late at night. He was a thin, blond, intense fellow, always chain-smoking. We would talk and talk, and in a while I would stretch out on my cot as he carved away at his tight surrealistic book about Montreal street life, writing in longhand on canary copy paper. It would be his only published work. In 1971, when returning to Toronto from his native Sherbrooke, he lay down on the railway tracks at Port Hope and was killed by a CN train. He was twenty-six.

Almost exactly two years later, Harold Sonny Ladoo, another of the writers in whose future Anansi had such faith, was found murdered in a ditch in Trinidad, where he'd returned on some family business. He had published one book, *No Pain Like This Body*, and left another, *Yesterdays*, which would come out posthumously; he would also inspire Dennis to one of his most powerful poems, "The Death of Harold Ladoo." I believe I met Ladoo only once, when he was leaving the office of some editor as I was entering. He was twenty-eight. Later, another death shook Anansi's bones. John Thompson, a mysterious poet (who I always thought looked in photographs as Grey Owl would have looked without his aboriginal drag) also killed himself. Rumour linked his death to an Anansi love affair gone sour. But this was in 1976, long after my time, and I had no way of knowing what had happened.

Purely as a publishing idea, the most interesting of the Spiderlines was *A Perte de Temps*, because Anansi published it in French, untranslated, but with generous vocabulary notes and other helpful bits of encouragement for English readers, who Dennis felt, or hoped, would struggle through, reclaiming their old high school French as they went and emerging all the better for it. I'm not sure that the experiment as such was altogether successful. A flurry of translating between Quebec and English Canada had begun about 1960, but throughout the 1970s seemed to be interrupted by each new surge of separatist feeling. It wasn't really until the 1980s that writers from the two cultures began translating, publishing and reading each other on a limited scale out of a love of what they shared. Which, in the cases to which I refer—a group that includes Nicole Brossard, France Theoret and Louise Cotnoir in French, Daphne Marlatt, Sharon Thesen and Erin Mouré in English—was a specific interest in feminist poetics. But I think that *A Perte de Temps* did lead Anansi to commission translations, most notably from Sheila Fischman, of a lot of Quebec writing. The author who benefited most was Roch Carrier, whose first book with the press, *La Guerre, Yes Sir!*, was another of Anansi's hardy perennials and the start of Carrier's enduring popularity in English Canada.

La Guerre had not yet appeared at the time of the

Anansi party, but contact had been made, offers were in the offing, because one of my most vivid memories of the evening is of Dennis, upstairs at the end of the first-floor bannister, telling a very long and highly complicated joke. When I joined in, he was telling it, in French, to Roch and, in German, to some German-speaking person whose identity I never learned, all the while switching from French to German to English, without losing anyone's comprehension or missing a beat. The other reason the party is memorable to me is that I met a young English woman who was a university student and wrote poetry. She seemed to me quite wonderful, largely because I inferred she thought I might have possibilities as well. Her name was Sarah.

———

In France, Dave had met up with two other Canadian writers, the novelist Jim Bacque, ruggedly handsome and socially prominent, and the sometime poet and sometime fiction writer Roy MacSkimming, a very accessible fellow whom I'd met when he was an editor at Clarke, Irwin (and who would fill every conceivable type of job in the book industry down through the years). Together, the three of them had resolved to start a new press, which they would call new press, lower case. Dave was definitely finished with Anansi. He'd leave all that to Dennis and pursue a less literary but, considered as publishing, rather more imaginative list. And new press, located a short distance along Sussex Avenue on the other side of Spadina, near enough for the address to be a taunt, would do some very interest-

ing trade publishing while it lasted. In a few years
Maclean Hunter invested in the company, later increasing its holdings but finally disposing of the business to
the General Publishing group, run by Jack Stoddart Sr.
By that time Dave had already founded a third publishing company, Press Porcépic, which he later moved to
Victoria when he went there to teach. Porcépic would
change its name to Beach Holme after first spawning a
hugely successful software company.

The Godfreys' return from France coincided with
the Willimans' departure for Italy (Dan had got a grant
from the Canada Council to work in the Vatican
Archives), and suddenly I was told I couldn't sleep in
the basement anymore: I had to find some other place
to live. I didn't have to go far. I took a furnished room
atop the Williams Funeral Home, right next door. Later
I would joke about this with Bob Flanagan, another of
the Anansi poets. He lived not atop but beneath a former undertaker's on Dupont, in what had been its
embalming room. The floor was on a slant and there
was a large drain in the centre.

Looking back on it now, I can see clearly how
Anansi went through all the stages I have since seen
repeated in other presses. How initial success caused the
company to over-expand. How, in order to utilise its
new capacity efficiently, it briefly took on distribution
of other people's books (those of Coach House, in this
instance) only to find that efficiency, as such, was the
last result that should ever have been expected. Mostly
what I see, however, was the growing uneasiness all
round. Self-absorbed as I was, I couldn't help but sense
acutely that we were all going through our respective

sticky patches. Dennis captures the mood of exhaustion perfectly in his poem "Sibelius Park," which he had printed as a broadside at Coach House. The title came from the green space and playground across from his house on upper Brunswick. He wrote of himself in the third person hauling his body towards home every night with a feeling of desolation.

> *Rochdale Anansi how many*
> *routine wipeouts has he performed since he was born?*

I can't read it even now without recapturing the sense of fatigue everybody felt—he most of all, no doubt—at putting so much energy into making and selling "fine iconic books" in such piteously small numbers while the important human issues seemed to slip away in the lethal fog of the events in Vietnam. His mood, I believe, was made even bleaker by fissures in his marriage, though there was certainly no mistaking that politics was corroding all the surfaces of life for people with literary or artistic personalities. The poem speaks of "the grim dungeon with friends—men with/ deep combative egos, ridden men, they cannot sit still, they go on brooding…" I always assumed that he intended me to feel included in this reference—though not a me I'd honestly recognize now, with all my combativeness long since gone.

Anansi had a system for paperwork (I don't know whose invention it was—probably Dave's) which I've used ever since in whatever office I've had. There were three trays marked TODAY, TOMORROW and PROBLEMS. Some of the problems could be thorny—lost shipments, angry authors, production nightmares—and everyone had a quota of them to tackle. The biggest problem of all turned out to be Allen Ginsberg's *Airplane Dreams*. This was 1969, the year before the United Church sold the Ryerson Press to McGraw-Hill and set in train a series of political responses that would echo for almost twenty years. But thanks in no small part to Anansi, publishing Canadian books, and building a permanent audience for them, was already a defiant act, and a certain political infrastructure had begun to assume shape. One of the red flags for Canadian publishers was the so-called Manufacturing Clause of the American copyright law. This was a measure aimed at protecting U.S. book printers from foreign competition. It held that the copyright on books by American citizens printed outside the United States would be lost if more than 3,000 copies were imported for sale into the U.S.

Dennis took complete charge of the Ginsberg once I brought in the manuscript; except for arranging for the author's cover photo to be taken and a few other small chores, I had nothing to do with the project, as my duties had always been of a more general office character, with some fulfilment and promotion thrown in. What's more, the book materialized during the period when Dave and Dennis were splitting up. Which is to say, at the point when Dennis was at some pains to show himself and others that he had keen commercial instincts or at least a certain familiarity with the practical end of life. He decided to print 6,000 copies of the book—a bigger print order than other Anansi books by a factor of six. True, Ginsberg's *Howl* had sold far more than 100,000 copies at that stage, but it was his major work, which *Airplane Dreams* hardly was, and in any case had sold them over a thirteen-year period. (When Coach House published Ginsberg's *Iron Horse* in 1973, it brought out its normal and prudent 500 copies, later going back to press for another 500.) I wasn't encouraged to voice an opinion. The reason the Anansi run was so large is that Dennis had made Anansi's first foreign distribution agreement, or thought he had. Flexing his entrepreneurial muscles, he had cut a deal with Ferlinghetti at City Lights to take most of the run.

Airplane Dreams needed one of Anansi's "sheepish errata," as Dennis would call them in "Sibelius Park." It took the form of a bookmark, and on the other side of it Dennis took it on himself to denounce the Manufacturing Clause, proclaiming that 5,000 copies of this work were being shipped across the border in defiance of the offensive American law. I'm not sure whether Ferlinghetti really understood the dangers or whether the author did either, though Dennis's little manifesto on the bookmark said the challenge was being made "with Allen Ginsberg's permission." In any case, the inevitable happened. The shipment was seized by U.S. Customs. Dennis was summoned to offer his defence and argue why the books should not be destroyed as contraband. He had no defence, so they were.

Poor Ferlinghetti, already chary of Canadians over non-payment of all the books sent up to Harry Fine on credit, vowed never again to do serious business with Canadian publishers, as I believe he has not, though he and Dennis worked out a joint-imprint edition of *Airplane Dreams* the following year to save face and assuage the author.

Shortly after this, Dennis asked me to come have a coffee with him at the Varsity Restaurant up on Bloor Street, an Anansi hang-out a few doors down from Meyer's Cigar Store where he bought his cigarillos every day. He promptly amazed me by saying I was fired. He didn't phrase it that way, explaining instead that he was bringing about a major reorganization and expansion of the press in which he didn't feel he could keep me on. In fact, he did just what executives are always taught never to do; he told half a dozen other people that he was firing me and gave all of them different reasons. I knew from the moment he finished the fatal pronouncement that I was the scapegoat for all the money lost on the Ginsberg fiasco. I felt as though all the air had been suddenly vacuumed out of my chest cavity, *swoosh*. But I recovered, as I always did. True, I had no money and wondered how I was going to feed myself. But then again I was twenty and it was time to turn the page and do something that would give me more opportunity to get on with my own writing. I've never harboured the least resentment against Dennis as I've followed his career appreciatively down through the years from a short distance away (for though we both moved any number of times we still seem to wind up in the same old neighbourhood). My regret is only that, after the Anansi days as during them, I was never able to communicate with him as effectively as I would have wished. I'm careful not to say that *we* can't communicate well, for it's my transmitter and not his receiver that's faulty somewhere. It saddens me.

As for Anansi, the story can be wrapped up quickly. Dennis was not a successful or happy manager, and the press was soon under the presidency of Shirley Gibson, who had been involved with the theatre and was the estranged wife of Graeme Gibson. One of the books she published was her own, a first collection of poetry. Then Margaret Atwood, who had commenced her loving partnership with Graeme Gibson, became more heavily involved in the press. Another of those interested was Ann Wall, who later bought out all the minority shareholders, including the ones like me with only a few shares. She had come to Canada long ago with a draft-aged husband, who had been an early Anansi volunteer. Peggy Atwood's former husband, Jim Polk, a talented and pleasant man with advanced degrees in both English and music, then became the editor of the press, which by this time had long since left Spadina, first for a house near the CBC on Jarvis and later for a co-operative publishers' building on Britain Street, a little spit of a street around Sherbourne and Queen.

The Anansi books in this later period, through the 1970s and well into the 1980s, were much better chosen, better edited and better designed than the early ones—mostly thanks to Polk, I believe. The range continued to be broad, and the trend, already apparent, of showing more verve in fiction than in verse was exacerbated. And there were a few more bestsellers, such as Atwood's *Survival,* though of course bestsellers were never really the point. Social comment, the third force on its list, had always been a ragged, haphazard affair under the original team. Now, under Gibson, Wall, Atwood and Polk (later reduced to Wall and Polk), it took on a fresh sense of purpose: more realistic in its causes, more practical, more consistent. But for all that, Anansi books never again seemed so important.

This is not a trick of perspective from my own vantage point, but the fact that the publishing landscape, thanks partly to Anansi's efforts but to a lot of other people's as well, had changed fundamentally—and for the better, so far as Canadian books were concerned. There were now Canadian publishers galore who were more or less small and to some degree commercial or non-exclusionary. As a result, Anansi's books were no longer big events. They didn't get into so many stores or get so many reviews. Even people like me who paid strict attention to these matters could discover some interesting Anansi book by chance, years after its publication. In growing up, Anansi was somehow diminished. In 1989 Ann Wall sold the imprint to Jack Stoddart Jr., son of the man who had bought out new press. There were no sad obituaries.

The general feuding of Anansi's vital if immature years dragged on in people's memories, of course. When the Godfreys were settled permanently in Victoria, Ellen, to some people's surprise, I think, began to write mysteries and true-crime books. Her first detective story was set in a small publishing house where a young bearded poet lived in the basement. The fictional murderer bore a strong resemblance to Dennis Lee.

CHAPTER FOUR

CHILD-OF-LETTERS

S ARAH LIVED in Rosedale. Her place was at the
south end of Glen Road, close to the ravine and the
Sherbourne Street Bridge. It was in a former mansion
that had been broken up into a dozen or more bed-
sitting rooms, all occupied by young women of quality.
On that, her landlady insisted. Sarah was studying creative writing at York University, and in her own time
read Victorian novels. When I knew her, for instance,
she was pushing her way through the oeuvre of Harrison Ainsworth, the low-grade Sir Walter Scott whose
romances, like *Old St Paul's* and *Tower of London*,
focused on individual buildings. For a dollar or so each,
she had picked up odd volumes of these, bound in
quarter-leather and with red marbled end-papers, at
Old Favourites, the big secondhand bookstore on University Avenue. The books always lay scattered on her
mantle-shelf. She was the kind of person to whom having a mantle-shelf seemed right. As such, she was certainly living in the perfect house.

I found the coziness, the human comfort and the
bookishness a narcotic combination, especially during
dark or rainy days, when we would stay in bed together,

reading for hours. Sometimes she would read aloud—
she had a beautifully modulated middle-class English
voice, not too plummy and never arch. Sometimes we
would even exchange books back and forth between us.
I can still remember many of the titles we consumed
together there. In fact, despite decades of moves and
other traumas, I can still put my hands on some of the
actual copies.

We had a slight problem with her landlady, Mrs.
Kemeny, who frowned on male visitors. Once, after a
particularly literary evening, we awoke in the morning
to noises in the corridor. The other residents, wearing
their dressing gowns, were shuffling up and down the
carpet runners, queuing at the bathrooms with tooth-
brushes in their hands. Soon there was the shrill Hungarian voice of Mrs. Kemeny, getting nearer. Sarah went
out to mingle with the others while I activated the
emergency plan we had devised long before. I left by the
window. From the nearly horizontal portion of the
downspout that ran along the side of Sarah's room, it
was only a short drop to the ground.

I had a problem with my own accommodations as
well: I couldn't very well go on living at the funeral
home next door to Anansi. So I began a campaign to
convince Sarah that we should find a place of our own
and move in together. Depending on the mood, I presented this as a plan that was either ruggedly practical or
a romantic inevitability. She was reluctant to give up her
cocoon-like space, reluctant even more to commit to
me, but she promised to give the thing a try. As we
didn't have much money even after pooling our
resources, yet wanted something large and airy, the

search proved tiresome. At one point we were lucky and almost had an apartment in one of those 1920s buildings up the Avenue Road hill towards St. Clair, all light brown brick and leaded windows, but the landlord who was showing us the place overheard some remark Sarah made to me that betrayed my place of birth, and he suddenly grew hostile, saying he didn't rent to Yankees.

In the end we were rescued by Sarah's younger sister, Holly. She lived with a dope dealer on St. Nicholas Street, a strange combination of warehouses and residential buildings that ran north/south between Yonge and Bay, from Wellesley all the way to Charles. Or rather she had been living with him for a while but they were now breaking up. Anyway, she knew the two-bedroom across the hall was coming on the market. It was only $110, utilities included. So what if the plumbing didn't usually work? Sarah was sceptical— because, I thought, she didn't approve of her kid sister's paramour. In fact, I was pressuring her into an arrangement she wasn't ready for or didn't totally believe in.

One day while Sarah was at school, I moved all my stuff over from Spadina, using the subway. This took much of the morning and the whole afternoon. By the time of the last trip I was carrying only my bed, which was a big five-inch-thick slab of foam from the army surplus store. It was getting on towards rush hour now, and I had the foam doubled over in my aching arms, like a dancing partner. Inevitably, other passengers pushed, the subway pitched and yawed, and the damn thing got away from me, striking a fat lady in the ass and knocking her across the aisle, shades of Groucho, Harpo and Chico.

But that night, when I offered to help Sarah start moving her stuff as well, I found out that she hadn't actually begun to pack. In fact, she hadn't even given her notice to the loud Mrs. Kemeny. We had what felt like long talks—one endless discontinuous talk, it seemed to me—the result of which was Sarah's conclusion that I couldn't communicate, and she didn't mean my speech impediment. I wouldn't admit it then, but of course I came to see that she was right—like to think that I knew it even then but was suppressing what I didn't wish to recognize. Anyway, she moved a few, a very few, of her things to St. Nicholas Street. Still, I could never get her to stay the night there with me. She would come almost every day and see Holly to comfort her during her travails, and even put aside her disdain of the dope dealer long enough to help Holly pack. I tried to lend a hand but was told I wasn't needed. I knew I'd never see Sarah again once she had helped her sister move to some place she had found for her out the Danforth.

All of us, I believe, have rooms that we re-inhabit only in our dreams, where the layout and atmosphere are so totally familiar to us that we find nocturnal comfort there. For me, that space is 52 St. Nicholas Street, corner of Inkerman. Some imposter of a building now occupies this site, but in my time there was a four-storey H-shaped structure with bow windows in front, put up before the First World War. It was here I decided to stay on alone and try to make my way solely by writing, though the rent was more than I could afford. There is an exact twin of No. 52, doubtless the work of the same builder, elsewhere in the city, and I always make a point of going out of my way to pass by. Whenever I do, I smile.

I was on the second floor. Immediately below me were two nursing students whose real interests were making sculptures out of old surgical devices. Their place was filled with them, and some hung in the window, causing passersby to wonder. As for Holly's former boyfriend across the hall from me, he kept his apartment dark with what I imagined might be blackout curtains from the Second World War, using only candles for illumination. Sitar music played constantly, and the stale air, thick with incense, would sometimes be enlivened by the tinkling of chimes, which hung suspended from all the doorways and window-frames—a crude security system, I guessed. His cover was that he worked a couple of nights a week as a teacher of English to new immigrants. This was ironical, as he himself was only recently arrived from Merseyside and spoke the thickest, most incomprehensible Scouse I had ever heard: a matter not of accent alone but of a vocabulary understood only within a certain section of Liverpool. The speech of John Lennon, when he was off-stage and tired, tended in this same direction, as I found out when I interviewed him around this time during one of his Toronto visits, but was not impenetrable to remotely the same degree. Several months into my life there, I noticed, as who could not?, that the building was suddenly being staked out. Some nights two male caucasians with beefy shoulders and little hats would spend hours across the street in an unmarked four-door sedan with a whip antenna and no dealer's decal. As they took no pains to be subtle, I assumed their presence was intended to rattle someone out into the open. To my surprise, they proved not to be after my neighbour but a young guy I'd never actually seen who lived holed up on the ground floor, in a little room far at the back, in what I suppose must once have been the custodian's quarters. It seems he was a fellow fugitive, wanted in the States for I forget what violent crime. The In the Courts column of the *Tely* had all the details.

Visitors were always coming and going at St. Nicholas, and one day Michael Ondaatje stopped by with a camera round his neck. He was in one of those periods, which his many friendly critics have tended to downplay, of wanting to be a photographer, a playwright and a filmmaker, or at least of wanting to mix any or all of those callings with his poetry and fiction (as he would in fact do with such success). He took some shots of me inside the apartment. But I never saw them and now he says they're undoubtedly lost.

Like most every poet for the preceding couple of generations, I made one of my first periodical appearances in the *Canadian Forum*, then being edited by Milton Wilson, and kept adding, one by one, the credits of such little magazines as would have me. I also had an early patron in Bob Weaver, a kindly anecdotal sort of man who ran the literary department of CBC Radio and was also editor of the *Tamarack Review*, the quarterly with in those days the widest and deepest moat (though this began to change not long afterwards). Bob's preferred method of doing CBC business was an annual coffee at the Four Seasons Hotel, across Jarvis Street from the Radio Building. There he would clean and re-clean his pipe and tell you his latest warm and

affectionate story about Morley Callaghan or Margaret
Laurence and behave in a generally circumlocutory way
until the end of the meeting. Then, sometimes while
rising to find his coat, he would let drop that he would
buy such and such a batch of poems or this or that short
story for broadcast.

I was not averse to picking up small jobs from book
publishers either. In the basement of a building on
Inkerman Street, a few doors away from my apartment,
was Peter Martin Associates, one of the earliest of the
generation of small presses which later, when Anansi
came along to give definition and train a pool of transient talent, came to be seen as the Anansi generation.
PMA, as it was called, was run by the husband-and-wife
team of Peter and Carol Martin, then in their early thirties, I suppose, who put out a big list of general-interest
books. Their publishing sprang originally from their
book club, the only one for Canadian titles exclusively,
which they had started in 1959 and were still pursuing,
along with *Canadian Reader*, a magazine for the members. Their books had a small-l liberal and sometimes
even a civil libertarian slant to them, which I liked, but
dealing with Peter was difficult. Carol was invariably
kind, solicitous, knowledgeable, friendly and efficient—qualities she later carried with her, following
their divorce, to her roles as a Canada Council arts officer and then as a publishing consultant. Peter had neither her taste in Canadian writing nor her likable
personality. What's more, he was impractical in business matters. He kept an enormous staff, largely, I
think, because it made him feel successful, but too few
of the books he published ever found their way into

enough stores to support the kind of place he ran. He was also, like many alcoholics, a bully. Whenever he and I talked, he would manage to work into the conversation the fact that he had attended all the best private schools and I had not. My retort, which I always managed to keep from saying out loud, was to ask why if, as he claimed, he'd gone to all these places, he hadn't been taught proper manners. So I tried to deal mostly with Carol, and as such edited a poetry anthology for them and wrote prefaces to a few of their other books.

I tried never to turn away hack work if it had some connection to books and the arts, and while I never invested such jobs with more seriousness than they deserved, I never looked down on them either. I offer two examples to stand for the many. At *Maclean's*, which was then still a general-interest magazine and not yet a news weekly, the end of the budgetary year coincided with the approach of spring, and the editor, Peter Newman, was to some extent reduced to living off his inventory, like a householder using up all the leftovers in the fridge in the last week before payday. Throughout the year, the magazine had been sending top-notch photographers like John De Visser back and forth across the country on assignment; the result was now a lot of expensive transparencies which, though already paid for, had never, for one reason or another, been used. Staff members at light-tables in the art department kept arranging and re-arranging them in different combinations, trying to find a common theme. There were Atlantic fishermen working their nets. There were Ontario farmers preparing the ground for ploughing. There were extreme close-ups of dew drops on the leaves of weeds somewhere on the Prairies. So it was decided to run these all together as a tribute to spring in Canada. There was room for a certain precise amount of text—say, 2,435 words—to run like a serpent around the various images, and for some reason it was decided to have me interview Marshall McLuhan about the place of spring in the Canadian psyche. They could hardly have come up with a celebrity less obviously interested in the role of spring, or anything else, as it applied to the Canadian psyche.

I tracked down the famous reeve of the Global Village, the great guru of mass media, at the special institute bearing his name at the University of Toronto. With mounting embarrassment, I explained the premise. He remained silent for what seemed the longest time, and I thought certain our interview had ended before it had got under way. Then suddenly he said words to the effect of "OK, kid, take this down." Whereupon he switched on his fountain of wonderful nonsense and out came a stream of something very much like prose, all quite fresh-sounding and superficially deep, exactly 2,435 words' worth of it. He then bade me good morning. The money pains at the magazine turned out to be nothing more serious than gas, so I was paid off and the piece never ran.

At this time I had some friends at the madhouse called McClelland & Stewart, and I was not too proud to take unsolicited manuscripts from the slush pile to be read and reported on for as little as ten dollars each. The relationship led to one of my more bizarre bits of editorial troubleshooting. Peter Taylor, a former novelist on the M&S list who had become the company's marketing manager, phoned me in a panic to say that the bright young person they had taken on as a copywriter and of whom they had entertained high hopes had let them down by having a nervous breakdown or some such. Anyway, could I write all the copy for the autumn catalogue by Monday morning? I pointed out that this was Friday and that I hadn't read any of the books. No problem, Peter replied cheerily; in many cases, there were rough notes from some of the editors saying what the works seemed to be about. And anyway, he went on, we'll pay you—and he named what sounded to me an impossibly large sum of money.

By simply working through the night for two nights running, I had the job done by Sunday. I was ready to defy anyone, even the poor authors, to recognize that in most cases I didn't have the foggiest idea what I was talking about. I grew so cocky, in fact, that I used Sunday to write a satire on the process of writing fall catalogue copy. One of the autumn titles, I remember, was a sumptuous book on Alfred Pellan's art. The real copy began something like this: "No expense has been spared in the fidelity of the reproductions of these seventy-five works by the master of Quebec surrealist painting between the wars…" My translation into truth would have begun like this: "Jack McClelland was in Harry's Bar in Venice and he met this Italian printer…" I completed these rival versions for all the books in the catalogue, and on Monday morning called a courier to take the two sets off to M&S in a single package. I then waited for weeks with anxiety bordering on panic to see whether, in their haste, the company might have printed the wrong ones. Stranger things happened at

McClelland & Stewart in those days, much stranger.

When, in a celebrated political event around this time, the provincial government bailed the company out by guaranteeing some major bank loans, the politicians naturally imposed a stipulation on the deal: the right to appoint the M&S chief financial officer. My friends were terrified that the person from Clarkson Gordon would arrive in his three-piece suit and instantly eliminate all the fun and freedom that made their work there bearable, even enjoyable. Some months later I happened to be at the offices, and was expecting to see all my buddies with short hair and suits. Instead I saw the dreaded person in question. He was wearing a string of beads. This was the first sign that instead of Clarksongordonizing McClelland & Stewart, he himself had been McClellandized.

Most of the book publishers were still downtown in those days, having not yet fled to Don Mills, Richmond Hill or Markham (as they would do in the mid-1970s, only to return a decade later, at least their editorial and publicity departments). McClelland & Stewart may have been divided, with its main shop on Hollinger Road in East York and most of its editorial and design people downtown, at King and Simcoe Streets, above a place called Speedy Auto Glass. But the others were fully integrated at their individual locations. For example, according to one of my feeble witticisms of the time, Macmillan was *in* Bond Street while Doubleday was *on* Bond Street. Most of the magazines, too, were located in what, until the Great Fire of 1904, had been the printing and commercial arts district whose main thoroughfares were Adelaide, Richmond and Wellington Streets, an area that still retained traces of that heritage—primarily because the rents were cheap.

I had quite a ways to go before the big magazines would accept me as a regular, but every week I made my rounds. Checking the trap-line, as a friend calls it. My stops included two editorial offices a block from each other on Adelaide Street: that of *artscanada*, then a kind of thematic extravaganza, often surprising and usually late in appearing, and that of *Toronto Life*, which had commenced only in 1966 and was already on its third editor, a legendary character who wore moccasins in the office and carried a bullwhip. The owner of *Toronto Life* at the time was Michael Sifton, an Ontario member of the western newspaper-owning family, and the magazine seemed to reflect what a series of editors thought a wealthy amateur publisher would wish for. As a result, Sifton, who owned an indoor polo field and was an avid equestrian, had the pleasure of seeing the horsey set displayed in his magazine every month. That is to say, the magazine's sometimes embarrassing journalistic adolescence was bound up partly with trying to make the periodical reflect some veneer of sophistication that the city did not in fact then possess. *Toronto Life* had a society editor: an effervescent, prematurely blonde woman who emitted some faint suggestion of perhaps once having been a Hungarian. She and one of the magazine's photographers would show up at parties and openings, taking down names and snapping pictures. I cherish the memory of the cutline beneath a photograph of a certain cultural figure of my acquaintance. The caption ran, in its entirety: "Here's perky Sandra, hosting a visiting Peruvian!"

By now, I was well underway on my lifelong policy of trying to continue my education through book-reviewing. They didn't know it, but I used literary sections of papers and magazines to subsidize my studies while earning myself a pittance in the bargain (a kind of student loan, doled out fifty or seventy-five dollars a throw, which never had to be paid back). As time went on, I grew more not less ambitious in reviews, until I thought nothing of reading four or five other books if necessary to deal adequately with the one at hand, and I came to dislike reviews that attempted to slide by on a reviewer's subjective opinion—book good, me like; book bad, me no like—without always comparing every possible facet to that of some other book or writer and without trying to deal with ideas. No reviews without ideas, this almost became a battle cry. A few people tolerated the kind of reviewing I was interested in developing, but seldom for very long. I found a thousand ways to disguise serious intent, as a baby's parents learn to hide green vegetables in other foods they know won't be spit out.

The three daily newspapers were important stops on my trap-line: the *Star* at the famous address 80 King Street West, where I would sometimes pause in the Stoodleigh Restaurant downstairs to gather my will or have a shoe shine at the barber shop next door to make myself less unprepossessing; the *Globe and Mail*, a bit farther along King, at the corner of York; and the *Telegram*, down on Front, just west of Spadina, its new building, which the *Globe* would later get for itself like a hermit crab taking over another's vacated shell. I was happiest at the *Star*, whose liberal politics were then still pretty firmly intact, and several people were particularly nice to me, including Nathan Cohen, the famous drama critic and mythomane, though his severe countenance scared me to death. But the *Globe* was more receptive to the kind of reviewing I wanted to do, and could give me almost as many books as I could ingest. It was a strange place, however, with odd sensitivities—and sometimes very limited space. When the autobiography of the White Russian novelist Nina Berberova was first published in English, in 1969, I wrote a short and, in retrospect, stupid notice of it. Within days, the author had dispatched a reproving personal letter to Dic Doyle, the *Globe*'s editor. Bill French, the editor of the books section, warned me that Doyle was rumoured to be impressed with the letter's logic. For the next several weeks I came and went by the *Globe*'s back door in Pearl Street and wrote under imaginative yet opaque pseudonyms. In those days I often had to use pseudonyms to survive. Custom said that one couldn't review for both the *Globe* and the *Star*, for example. But while writing in the *Globe* as Fetherling, I also, with the connivance of French's rival, Kildare Dobbs, wrote in the *Star* as Ronald Upjohn. No one was any the wiser until Upjohn launched a scathing attack on Fetherling one week. In any case, I was delighted when, twenty-two years later, Phillipe Radley's translation of the Berberova memoirs was republished, and I was able to write a long and better-considered piece on it.

As for the *Telegram*, the organ of an older Toronto, with roots in the Conservative Party and a WASP identity that few had seemed to question until well after the Second World War, one might have expected that its book coverage would be similar to that of, say, the Montreal *Star*, where John Richmond, the influential literary editor, could be counted on to review any books about the royal family and related concerns. But in fact, the *Tely* had a thoughtful and cosmopolitan book page presided over by Barry Callaghan, whose father, Morley, was the city's senior literary figure. The joke was always that if John Bassett, the proprietor, learned that he had a book page, he would have been cross. I never broke into the page at the *Tely* but hung about all the same, as I did at the other two papers, hoping for whatever crumbs of other writing might be going begging; but my links with the *Telegram*'s culture and aesthetic, so to call them, were never sympathetic, as with the *Globe*'s, nor organic, as with the *Star*'s. I met John Bassett only once, for example, and was impressed by the fact that his jaw-line was a perfect right angle, making him look as though he had been drawn by Milton Caniff (whose comic strip "Steve Canyon" appeared in the *Star*). Also, I couldn't help but observe that, though it was only four in the afternoon, he was wearing a tuxedo.

Even more so than later, publishers took an I-shot-an-arrow-into-the-air approach to publicity by sending out scores of review copies and hoping for the best. The review slips always gave Saturday release dates because Saturdays the newspapers' review pages appeared (there being no Sunday papers then). Such dates were broken at one's peril. Consequently, there was considerable competition to review new books on time, rather as new plays are reviewed, and just as in the theatre, there were parties to mark the occasion. Macmillan often threw sedate little parties with sherry, M&S sometimes lavish ones at exotic locations, such as the floor of the stock exchange or some rich person's roof garden. In September and October there might be several soirées a week, allowing a young reviewer, trying to get by in a world he never made, to exist almost entirely on gin and canapés. The saving in groceries, combined with the couple of dollars the review copies fetched in the secondhand bookstores, might permit him a badly needed scuttleful of coal.

Of those parties at which I was conscious, the one that sticks in my mind was a terribly posh affair thrown by Doubleday for their dreary money-spinner Arthur Hailey. It was at the old Granite Club on St. Clair Avenue and no doubt cost $40,000 or so in today's money. A poor commissionaire, stationed at the entrance, questioned the identity of two of the arriving guests, who turned out to be the all-powerful industrialist E.P. Taylor and his wife; the commissionaire was never heard from again. I remember meeting at that function a person who was already one of my favourite perennial fellow guests. He was a second- or third-string Toronto *Star* reviewer and entertainment writer who as a child had lived in the Ritz in London where his father had been head pastry chef and where one of his father's apprentices, drawn from the foreign-student quarter, was the young Ho Chi Minh. The war in Vietnam was still on the lips and in the lungs when the scene I describe took place, and hearing my *Star* friend let drop this autobiographical gem (which he did at every such occasion), a number of people gathered about him, pumping his hand with real emotion and pressing him for whatever memories of the great man, however small, he might possess. His response was to grab another fistful of crab puffs from the next waiter who floated by. "Not like Uncle Ho's," he would say. "His crusts were, well, *superb.*"

As a salesman of myself, I left almost everything to be desired. One old editor confided to me recently that when I first called on him in those days, his secretary tried to discourage him from seeing me, but he remembered a boy in his class at Upper Canada College who had stuttered and so decided to risk it. Yet I persisted. When I think back to this time in my life, it is always to grey days in winter, when the afternoon is shrinking into dusk and I'm getting more and more depressed as I bang on doors and have endless cups of coffee and make my case for myself and then go home in the dark to begin the little bits of work I've managed to secure. Sometimes I would be out from early in the morning and not return until after six, so I wouldn't know until the evening what had arrived in that day's post. Once I can remember coming home with a bag of Chinese food for dinner and pausing at the mail-box in the lobby to find a $250 cheque which I hadn't been expecting. Anyone who thinks this too trivial an anecdote to include has never been a freelance writer—or an independent writer, as I preferred to think of myself. Thus did I sidestep a term I disliked, one I associated with people of base purpose (who, parenthetically, were also much more successful at it than I was—a connection I couldn't quite see). If one can't be independently wealthy, I seemed to be saying to myself, at least one can be independently poor, but in any event, bloody independent. By being an independent or non-aligned writer, I meant more or less what a small freeholder means who tells you that mixed farming is best and wants no truck with agribusiness. It was a moral choice, if maybe also a moral choice one had forced on oneself as by some quirk of personality.

November 1987, almost twenty years later, early in the afternoon. I was packing to leave Toronto, trying to decide what I should take to Kingston, where I was to spend most of each week writing a books-and-ideas column for the *Whig-Standard*. Suddenly there was a savage banging at the door. Ruben Zellermayer was a sculptor who lived and worked in the basement of the adjoining house where I would sometimes see my old friend Gwendolyn MacEwen. He was in a state approaching shock.

"Gwen's dead," he blurted out. As he told me of finding the body at her apartment, he was actually rubbing his head back and forth in his hands, as though to erase the image from his mind. The first person he thought to tell was Joyce Marshall, one of Gwen's writer friends who lived close by. Then he came to me.

He was so distraught that I didn't know how to handle him, so I walked him round the corner to my wife Janet's bookshop on Bathurst Street. She's much better at emergencies than I am, emotional ones in particular.

That night, of course, and frequently thereafter in the coming months, I fell to thinking about poor Gwen, not the one whose photograph Ruben hung at the entrance to his studio, but the vibrant, mysterious and not in the least crazy Gwen I'd first met at Anansi and got to know back in the St. Nicholas Street days. She was only forty-six when she died, so she had to have been twenty-seven when I met her in 1968. Our first conversation was about the fact that I had been using the name Gwendolyn in some of my poems—until then, I'd never actually met a Gwendolyn; I simply thought it was a lovely combination of syllables. She looked exactly as she did on the dust-jacket of her most recent poetry collection, *A Breakfast for Barbarians*. She was petite, as people then said, and had large sad eyes under striking black brows, and wore her hair in a flip. The clothes she was partial to were first of all simple. She once admitted a liking for a particular type of lisle stockings which, she said, could only be bought at some virtually clandestine shop which catered to Roman Catholic nuns. But her clothes were dramatic as well, with flowing sleeves and silk here, brocade there. Of her appearance, I should say that she was totally up-to-the-minute by virtue of being indebted, in some vague but absolutely unmistakable way, to a much earlier time. All this made her inadvertently stylish, as she knew but wouldn't deign to acknowledge.

Like the work of Northrop Frye, Jay Macpherson and so many others, Gwen's was often concerned with the intersection of myth and life (and in her case particularly, with magic and anthropology). But she stood apart from the others, in large part because she wasn't an academic. She was in fact an autodidact (maybe that's why she and I got along so well) who, despite scholarship offers, had dropped out of school at eighteen in order to write. At twenty, she was an important figure in the little Toronto bohemia whose centre was Gerrard Street Village, the one whose feeling, I think, is best evoked in the text Harold Town did some years later for a book on Albert Franck's painting. Gwen published two poetry chapbooks, *Selah* and *The Drunken Clock*. When she was twenty-two, Eli Wilentz of the 8th Street Bookshop in New York brought out her first novel, *Julian the Magician*. This represented quite an undertaking for his press, Corinth Books, which until then had published only short works by most of the major Beats, nothing ambitious and nothing far afield. That is to say, Gwen became an early literary star. But unlike many people who find their talents are fashionable when they're quite young, she didn't disappear from the scene later on, as soon as the fickle media found someone else.

She had *noticed* the attention all right, but I don't think she was fazed by it. There was probably no one else in Canada then writing poetry made of the same materials as hers—the deep sense of magic and its relation to personal history, for example—yet she touched many different groups and circles in ways you would expect only a more public sort of writer to do. Michael Ondaatje told me once how terribly important it was to the community of poets studying and teaching in Kingston in 1965 when she agreed to come to Queen's to read. And of course a lot of feminist writers would look back to Gwen as a kind of pioneer. They saw her, I believe, as someone who got her start just barely before their own time and wrote from some of the same concerns, though not necessarily in the same diction as themselves (it hadn't been coined) nor even from the same stance (not yet rediscovered). Margaret Atwood, for example, would be a loyal champion of Gwen and her work until the end—and beyond.

I can only speculate what it meant for Gwen to live out her life in the city that was the scene of her unpleasant childhood. She wasn't the sort of person to reminisce, but one gathered that her upbringing had been somehow desolate. She never mentioned her father, an alcoholic Scot, whom her psychotic mother had left in the early 1950s—that is, not until her final book, *Afterworlds*, published eight months before she died, in which she used a photograph "by the author's father, Alick MacEwen A.R.P.S. (1904–1960)." But her mother, Elsie, a Cockney, was around Toronto during the years I refer to, living for a time in what was then the Elmwood Hotel for Women. I went there once with Gwen. It smelled of impending death and was decorated here and there with potted palms that resembled pathological specimens. The Elmwood was the sort of place where English women who had left decent homes to come out to Canada between the wars ended up in a state of impoverished widowhood, wondering how life went wrong. It also housed recovering psychiatric patients. Years later, the building was taken over by one of the granddaughters of the first Lord Thomson, who redid it as an exclusive dining club and spa for executive women with too much money.

Gwen's closest relative was her sister, Carol, who lived near Eglinton and Weston Road in the Borough of York. For years, particularly when she was working intensely on complicated projects like *King of Egypt, King of Dreams*, her novel about the pharaoh Akhen-

aton, she would use her sister's place as an accommodation address, meeting acquaintances, if she had to meet
them at all, at a nearby drugstore soda fountain, which
appeared not to have changed in thirty years.

She had amazing talents, some of which the public
saw and others they didn't. She had genuine psychic
ability, for example. Once I was sitting silently, trying to
remember the title of a movie I had seen based on an
H.P. Lovecraft story. (Even now, I have to go look it up:
The Shuttered Room.) I hadn't spoken aloud about this,
not so much as a word, when Gwen came into the room
and said matter-of-factly, "The name on the mailbox is
Tierney." I nearly fell off my chair, for this was a line of
dialogue on which the horror plot turned. Better
known was her gift for languages, which served her well
both as a literary translator and as a traveller. It was typical of her, though, that her knack extended beyond the
romance languages or any one family of languages. For
example, she taught herself enough Arabic to translate
some Arabic writers (though the only fruits of this
study to be published was a collection of folk tales for
children, *The Honey Drum*).

As a young girl she had been a violin prodigy. So
once when we went to a party together and she wandered off to a serious corner, she picked up a guitar that
happened to be lying there and started trying to figure
out how to transpose what she knew to this foreign
instrument. When she started, she was holding it across
her lap like a dulcimer and using her long nails to strike
the strings. By the time we were ready to go, she was
holding, fretting and fingering it in the conventional
manner, and playing quite freely. This wasn't the sort of

thing she'd ever mention again; it was just done to pass the time. I had known her reasonably well before I discovered by chance that she'd recently taken up painting, had done a roomful of interesting work, and then stopped—for good. Literature was her calling.

She wrote single-mindedly, as a writer must, and was never much tempted by material comforts, as most people are as they get older. When she needed extra money, she wrote plays—I remember many radio plays, richly evocative but never in the least romantic, for Bob Weaver at the CBC, and a new translation of *The Trojan Women* for one of the middle-class subscription theatres. She also gave splendid poetry readings, wearing a frock and the perfect eccentric earrings, performing faultlessly for a half-hour or an hour without consulting her book, which she held unopened in her hand—a mere prop— and sometimes dispensed with entirely. Much later, she would do a term here or there as writer-in-residence, but she was never a careerist, and she never stopped writing poetry—and never stopped always trying to write much different poetry—even after she began publishing short stories, a travel narrative, all sorts of things. People would never associate her with the tradition, because she eschewed all its cant and self-importance, but she was in fact a genuine *femme des lettres*.

"Can I ask you a personal question?" I said to her once.

She laughed. "If not now, I don't know when." We were in bed at St. Nicholas Street at the time. It was somewhere between winter and spring. I remember there was a big storm kicking up outside.

"What's the story on you and Milt?"

Everyone who had been around the Toronto writing scene at the time seemed to have tales about the incongruous and, I gathered, disastrous marriage of Gwen and Milton Acorn, the foul-smelling poet and self-proclaimed proletarian. People had told me of their days together on Wards Island, of how the two of them danced naked in their garden like William and Catherine Blake. I was incredulous. I mean, this had been only about six years earlier. It seemed unthinkable that she could ever have been mated up with Acorn if he was anything like the Acorn of 1968 and later: a red-nosed, red-necked wreck of a fellow who wandered the streets talking to himself, shouting out insults, threatening people with injury or even death.

"It was a mistake," she said. "The mistake of my life. I was a teenager." In fact, she had been twenty-one or twenty-two, and he thirty-nine or forty. "It didn't even last a year. Later, we got divorced." She talked a little more about it, making it sound like a whim that turned into tragedy. The tragedy was mostly that Acorn, having somehow had the astounding good fortune to find a woman like Gwen in love with him, never recovered from the rebuke when it turned out that she wasn't. First he went into self-imposed exile on the West Coast. One often heard stories of his life there. An antiquarian bookseller in Vancouver once showed me the carbon copy of one of the strangest literary projects I could imagine: a collaborative poetry collection, never published of course, by Acorn and bill bissett. Anyway, Acorn had returned to Toronto only in the past couple of years, and at this stage was living in a cheap rooming house on Spadina Road. Soon he would find a permanent home at the Waverley Hotel, where men without work waited each day for the Fred Victor Mission to open and where people in the beverage room drank beer to see if they could forget who they were. All the while he nursed an incredible hatred towards Gwen, but it was, I think, a hatred he could never quite bring himself to believe, and he heaped calumny on her friends, probably including Bob Mallory, an artist who had hung around the Gerrard Street Village (and who later, for no apparent reason, insisted on being called Leo—and then, after another rebirth of some kind, Leo Revised). One of Acorn's poems read:

> *For a woman to get published in the Tamarack Review*
> *If she has a good husband, she must leave him;*
> *Write sad existential letters about he was so*
> *goddam noble*
> *She couldn't stand it, whilst laying the dirtiest*
> *bastard in town;*
> *Then send poems to the Tamarack Review*
> *More explicit than a marriage manual but not so*
> *passionate.*

Then, just as today, Acorn had his loyalists. Some of the tolerance he engendered in people was because of—as well as despite—his politics, which were those of a 1930s cartoon in the *New Masses*, crudely drawn and without much relevance to present agonies. But mostly of course the people who put up with him did so for the sake of his poetry. For it was a curious fact that unlike the other similar figures one could name in literary history—from Dr. Johnson's friend Richard

Savage to Maxwell Bodenheim to Julian Maclaren-Ross—Acorn in fact had a big talent (the sample quoted above notwithstanding). Not, I think, one supplemented by much intellect or one much improved on down through the years, but an original voice all the same, and it was a calling he was faithful to. Maybe at base it was that focus and commitment that Gwen and he had in common. Maybe she saw the very real danger of her talent (if not his too) being trampled by the realities of living with a crazy man. At least that was what I picked up between the lines as she talked.

Years later, after both of them were dead, Al Purdy told me the part of the story she left out, even between the lines. Al had always looked up to, and looked after, Milton, one of the heroes of their shared literary youth. People said Milton had been hurt in the war, that he had a plate in his head and drew a disability pension. I never knew the extent of the truth, except that he used to be a carpenter before he downed tools to write about the working man instead of being one. The Purdy house on Roblin Lake at Ameliasburg, the setting of many a poem by Al and any number of others, started out as a simple A-frame that Al and Milton had built together with their own hands, using secondhand lumber, in 1954. Al, in short, was Acorn's closest and oldest friend, which is to say, his most tolerant and forgiving one. It was to him, Al told me, that Gwen came, asking if he would give evidence as the co-respondent in the divorce case if called on. Al said he felt he had no choice but to agree. He also said he was certain that Acorn never found out about her request.

In some ways, Gwen was English Canada's Marie-

Claire Blais, if for no other reason than a shared precocity and range. The two were certainly friends, so that when Blais won the Governor General's Award for fiction for *Les manuscrits de Pauline Archange*, she invited Gwen and me to be her guests at the ceremony in Ottawa. We decided to make Rideau Hall the site of situational theatre and mock the occasion by dressing in a high Victorian manner appropriate to the general air of pomposity. Gwen more or less chickened out, but I wore a frock coat and also a top hat, which I delighted to hand to an attendant as we entered. Prime Minister Trudeau came to the reception afterwards, giving evidence of knowing who all the writers were if not perhaps having read the books, and he was very attentive to Gwen, with that dry-ice charm of his. The year was also memorable not so much because Hubert Aquin refused the award, as francophone writers were forever doing, but because Leonard Cohen declined as well, for his *Selected Poems*, or rather first declined, then accepted, then declined again, disdaining to attend any of the celebratory parties but showing up at one of them anyway.

About this time, Al Purdy put together a substantial collection of Acorn's new and old poetry, *I've Tasted My Blood*, and was trying to persuade the Ryerson Press to publish it. It duly appeared, and many of Acorn's sentimental or political boosters hoped it would win the Governor General's for works published during 1969. When the awards were made known, however, the prize for poetry in English was shared, by George Bowering, for *Rocky Mountain Foot* and *The Gangs of Kosmos*—and Gwendolyn MacEwen, for *The Shadow-Maker*. Personally, I thought *Rocky Mountain Foot* easily the most important of the three. In any event, anyone could have foreseen what Acorn's reaction would be. He had long taken delight in writing and saying vile things about Gwen—in that respect, nothing changed. From this point forward, however, he seemed to exist at ever greater odds with reality.

The whole matter of Acorn's book became a cause, and a contingent of his friends proposed to organize a public ceremony, a kind of anti-Governor General's Award, at which Milt would be fêted, toasted and presented with a medallion proclaiming him the People's Poet. The event—I remember it well—was held at Grossman's Tavern on Spadina. The room was jammed with poets and readers and hangers-on and a surprisingly large delegation of the media. Eli Mandel, a poet of Acorn's age but an irredeemably conventional middle-class academic one who taught at York, was the master of ceremonies. Mandel was one of those profs who managed, in a way that was not in the least paradoxical to writers of that time, to turn out both dry academic criticism and elegies for dead rock stars. On the day in question he was using his populist voice, though he had forgotten to change from his academic's clothes—an expensive turtle-neck and slacks. When the TV cameras rolled and the medal was slung around Acorn's neck, Eli grabbed the microphone, raised a clenched fist in the air and shouted, "All power to the people!" There were no *people* present, not in the sense he was using the word. If by some miracle, a faction similar to the Red Guards had chosen that moment to rise up, however, they would of course have had Acorn and Eli and the whole lot sent off to re-education camps immediately. But no, I'm being much too harsh on Eli, who was merely letting himself look foolish in what he thought was a good cause.

Many of the folks involved in this *affaire* were caught up in its anxieties, including George Bowering, whom the Acorn troops began attacking quite fiercely. In a letter to George at about this time, I made a weak jest, in an awkward and totally misguided attempt to lighten the mood. Under stress, as anyone would be in that situation, he easily misread this inarticulate expression of sympathy and, much to my very genuine sorrow, reacted badly. Emotions were running high anyway, because by this time the United Church had made its decision to sell Ryerson Press, for generations the hearthstone of Can lit, to McGraw-Hill, of all people. I remember being part of at least one mass meeting, but the protests took many forms, including a decision by a small number of Ryerson authors to abrogate their contracts. There was a fashion at this time among certain writers to declare that "copyright is obsolete," that creative work should be treated like an element of life, not like a commodity. Victor Coleman, for example, went through a period of pointedly declaring his published work outside the artificial construct of the Copyright Act. Acorn now joined in and went so far as to inform McGraw-Hill Ryerson, as the Canadian branch plant was rechristened, that he would refuse to accept any tainted McGraw-Hill money that might come due him from *I've Tasted My Blood*. The McGraw-Hill types, an untutored lot of business people, unsophisticated in literary matters, stupidly took him at his word and pocketed some reprint fees that came in for him. Al Purdy had to act as intermediary and get poor Acorn his money.

Gwen would enjoy another green period, different from her first bout of literary fame, and lasting the better part of a decade. She married again, to a singer, Nikos Tsingos, and they operated a Greek coffee house out on the Danforth that always seemed to be full of food and music and old friends. Except that it was noisy, it was a kind of salon, and she was in her element—the perfect backdrop for the antiquarian side of her personality. She naturally acquired an easy fluency in Greek, spoken and written, and began translating Greek writers and making trips to Greece, including the ones recounted in *Mermaids and Ikons*, a travel narrative Anansi later published, a book whose prose I've long admired for its beauty and control. Gwen had always been attracted to the Near East—a rare quality in Canadian writers up to that time, who had generally preferred Africa or Latin America; attracted not only in a romantic way, as reflected in her poems about T.E. Lawrence (spurred, I think, by an interest in the Turks), but visually and linguistically as well, and to Israel and Egypt alike. Greek culture, as well as being a new source of joy in itself, seemed to give her the imaginative boost she needed to bring together her various long-standing interests—mythology, illusion, harmony, richness of textures, magic (or should I say magick?). Her writing only improved still more as she got older, though the devils began to snap at her ankles.

I don't know how else to phrase it. I certainly don't know how to explain it. Sure, the marriage to Nikos ended eventually, and I'm certain she was lonely. To dwell on those facts would be simplistic, yet I can offer no better insight, only observations from ever more infrequent meetings. She grew puffy from drink and could be sharp and sour on occasion. Twice she telephoned and monologized for half or three-quarters of an hour, full of almost incoherent complaints about neighbours and others. At these times, she would express theories about their behaviour that seemed to me to border on the paranoid (though I use the term only as a layperson does). I think her circle generally grew much smaller and less rewarding, and one heard that she would take up with questionable characters (perhaps trying to relive something—that's as far as I would care to go in the direction of analysis).

I didn't know until quite recently how much her death affected me. I feel the pang strongly when I read certain of her books again and I'm warmed by the memory of the brief time we were in communication. I'm quick to add that I claim no special privilege of recollection. Many others knew her much better than I did and over a longer period. Yet she was always, I believe, the sort of person to keep her acquaintances in separate compartments—we spotted that in each other right away. There was, however, one friend we had in common, and in the first few days after Ruben brought the horrible news, I wrote a letter to Vera Frenkel, the video artist. She had been acquainted with Gwen at intervals since the early 1960s and had recently come to form a friendship with her. She was away in England at this time, as artist-in-residence at the Slade School, so I sat down to give her the facts as I'd learned them. I told her how Ruben

hadn't talked with Gwen since Saturday and, fearful that something might have happened, went to

her place on Major Street and let himself in with
the hidden latchkey. He quickly sensed tragedy and
found her body in the bedroom where she'd died
sometime in the previous 24 hours....

Janet had telephoned Gwen about a week earlier
but had got her during a bad spell (the DTs or verg-
ing on the DTs). Ruben says that for the last little
while she had been experiencing small stroke-like
episodes. It was apparently a larger version of the
same that killed her. She was dressed and had her
feet on the floor but her torso across the bed, as
though she had fallen while passing through the
room. She had been eating an apple. Certainly
there was no note or other evidence of suicide nor
any sign of foul play, though the cops apparently
believe somebody may have been in the apartment
before Ruben and left without notifying anyone.
Ruben reported that they were looking for a drinking buddy, a construction worker who'd been staying there a couple days.

What a bloody awful waste. As I say, I hate to be
the one to tell you but I'm certain you're not seeing
the *Globe* there (and the copies at Canada House
are always three weeks old in any case) and I
thought you'd want to know.

———————

In the last days before Sarah left me, or thought better
of me, she and I went to a party in a coach-house apart-

ment in the Annex. The hosts were an actress friend of hers I didn't know and her housemate, a square-jawed young journalist named Bill Cameron. In later years Bill would be one of the faces of the national news on CBC Television, but in those days he had two far less significant jobs, writing a column for the *Star Weekly*, then being edited by Peter Gzowski, and hosting, only temporarily as it turned out, a Sunday morning magazine show on CBC Radio. The column was called "Bohemia by Bill Cameron" and dealt with such matters as House of Anansi and the thousands of suburban kids and rubberneckers who thronged Yorkville every Friday and Saturday night, hoping to sight some hippies and smell an illegal fragrance. The radio show was called *Sunday Supplement* and was produced by Howard Engel, whom Bill introduced me to that evening. Howard was a gentle and urbane man in his late thirties who had recently come back to Toronto after freelancing for the Corporation in France and on Cyprus. He was an intensely literary fellow, interested mostly in the classic modernists but with broad tastes. He was married to Marian Engel, who had just then published her first novel, *No Clouds of Glory*.

When Sarah went out of my life, I was overcome, slowly but steadily and with worsening effects, by a state of depression. Not for the first time in my life nor the last, I felt like an old hard-hat deep-sea diver, moving along the ocean bottom in leaden boots. Both my own writing and my bread-work fell off, and I realized that if I were going to keep the place on St. Nicholas, with its luxury of the second bedroom to be used as an office, I had better get some sort of small base income that I could depend on every month to help with the rent. In quest of such an arrangement, I went up and down my trap-line, and importuned my contacts. Finally I was thrown back on making entirely new acquaintances for this purpose. It was in this spirit that I went to the CBC Radio Building one day and called on the poet Phyllis Webb, who was producing *Ideas*, the talks series she had originated a few years earlier. I was an admirer of her work, particularly the collection *Naked Poems*, and we chatted about poetry for a while before I explained my dilemma. While promising to consider me for freelance work in the future, she sent me over to see Howard (whom I think she also might have telephoned the instant I left her office). As luck would have it, Howard had just been down talking to Marty Ahvenus, proprietor of the Village Book Store in the old Gerrard Street Village, asking what was new and hot, and Marty had pressed on him a copy of my Anansi book. Never had timing worked more in my favour. It was clear I couldn't be a broadcaster (though in time I did manage to do a few bits of on-air work— they always involved long hours at the Ampex, painstakingly eliminating my strained pauses and repetitions with a single-edge razor blade). But there was a lot of miscellaneous writing and story-vetting to be done on a ninety-minute weekly magazine programme, and Howard gave me a short contract. That soon expired and was extended with another one, this time at a gross of $125 a week—more money than I had ever earned.

Thus, Howard Engel, a genial friend of writers and a frustrated writer himself (until, many years later, following his divorce and remarriage, he parted from the CBC acrimoniously and to support himself stepped up production of the mystery stories he had started to create, employing the durable character of Benny Cooperman). Howard made few demands and was quick to praise, and actually seemed to enjoy watching me build a kind of literary career partly on office time while making sure that I had a chance to meet or work with some of the figures in broadcasting history who were still around—people like Andrew Allan, the dapper little drama producer, and J. Frank Willis, the veteran news correspondent associated with the 1936 Moose River Mine Disaster and so many other big stories of the past. And Howard understood completely when, after I'd saved enough money from the munificent salary, I bid him adieu and moved to Vancouver for a time, while still keeping my place in Toronto—indeed, while still trying to maintain the illusion that I hadn't really left. This action would inevitably provoke some contradictory sightings by other people, but I found that I was following an impulse that has always been with me, to maintain places in more than one city, or at least to have post office boxes elsewhere and cash and clothes and supplies stashed in other venues where I could get to them quickly, always plotting silently how to escape the momentary pressures of the one for the fleeting pleasures of another: a sort of geographical bigamy without sex or intimacy, but only a certain amount of comfort of a different and solitary kind. I became a type of mental-health hypochondriac, you see, always fearful that I might be showing the first signs of slipping into my mother's psychosis. My vigilance was constant. So, starting later, I resolved instead to let Father's personality rise to dominance, especially in my dealings with what was proving the rough, knockabout world of writing, publishing and journalism. I was determined to treat others better than they treated me. My selfish reward, which was years even decades in taking effect, would be greater calm and a little self-assurance (but not necessarily an enhanced immunity to other people's stings). It was to heal myself that I hitchhiked to Vancouver on that occasion, and when I felt I was better I returned. I then pursued all the publishers and magazines and even the CBC with renewed dedication.

As I couldn't really sell myself—that is, my slick presentation of self, for I had none, but only the kind of awkwardness of manner that the naive often mistake for sincerity—I had to become a dealer in ideas instead, at both the wholesale and retail levels. I regularly gave or sold book and article ideas to writers or publishers, and I managed to make myself modestly useful as an outside assessor of ones generated by others. For this was a time, like all times, when a lot of flabby nonsense was in the air, masquerading as thought. I'm remembering a visit to Toronto by John Wilcock, the putative father of the underground press movement, and it was in that sense, I suppose, that Seymour Krim once wrote of him as one of the most important American journalists of his time. John was an Englishman, then in his mid-forties, who had worked in Toronto years earlier, first at British United Press and then at Jack Kent Cooke's Consolidated Press, which published *Saturday Night* and *Liberty* and a number of trade magazines, trying to rival Maclean Hunter. Then he went to New York where he founded the *Village Voice* with Norman Mailer and Daniel Wolf (his part always ignored or downplayed in historical retellings). Later he had a hand in starting the two most important American hippie papers as well, the *East Village Other* and the *Los Angeles Free Press*. He was an insatiable traveller now (and the anonymous author of Arthur Frommer's original *Mexico on $5 a Day*), and for years he'd been bumming about Europe, putting out a little alternative press digest called *Other Scenes*. Bundles of it would arrive from time to time, postmarked New York or Amsterdam, and stuffed as well with what the CIA called pocket litter—lewd matchbook covers, subversive political buttons, unintentionally hilarious foreign advertisements written in English by non-native speakers. One day he was back in Toronto and we were having a conversation in the CBC canteen when we bumped into Tuli Kupferberg. I sat back amazed as these two gentle souls fell to bickering, then loudly arguing, in rancorous earnest, about whether or not appearing on the *Tonight Show* with Johnny Carson was in and of itself, *ipso facto*, a counter-revolutionary act. This was a particular and rather hypothetical controversy I confess I hadn't heard before, though in later years I've seen references to the anguish it caused at the time among people like Neil Young.

Anyway, I was an idea-pedlar, but the best idea I had never saw the light of day. I remained full of fervour against the war in Vietnam, which still threatened to go on forever, but I was in the ironic position of finding it impossible to deal with other people who had fled the States for Canada. They didn't care about Canada, it appeared to me, and indeed a large portion of them returned "home" once they could. What's more, they seemed too full of rugged American individualism to be able to work collectively. These resisters were losing the publicity war in the States and lately in Canada, too, just as surely as the Americans were losing the fighting war in Vietnam. At this time, Islamic fundamentalism had not yet become the main source of anti-American agitation in the rest of the world. The role was performed instead by a variety of socialist states, particularly Cuba and Algeria, which harboured America's political refugees, people such as the brilliant prison-essayist Eldridge Cleaver, and otherwise supported those working inside and outside America against Washington's interests.

My idea was to hit up the Cubans and Algerians for a couple hundred thousand dollars—we could have done it, too; this was pocket change for them—to establish a media counter-offensive. The plan was to name a U.S. government-in-exile temporarily housed in Canada until the undemocratic war could be brought to a halt and free and fair elections held—in the States. We would find articulate and well-scrubbed young draft exiles from Oberlin College and other expensive schools to stand for election among their peers as president and vice-president. This would have been irresistible—irresistibly irritating and provocative—to the U.S. networks, the newsmagazines, the wire services and the big newspapers. My estimation was that the novelty would have worn off in a few months, but until then our leaders-in-waiting would be absolutely ubiquitous, giving the Movement an entirely new way of communicating the anti-war message—and probably generating enough donations not only to make the scheme self-supporting, but also to set up a relatively sophisticated propaganda campaign that would be aggressively proactive rather than merely passive and situational. The biggest obstacle, it seemed to me, was how to determine in advance whether the newly elected Trudeau government, so generally sympathetic to anti-American initiatives, would close down the operation under some quibbling provision of the neutrality statutes, or whatever other law the solicitor-general could find. I located reliable, well-placed people who made ever so discreet advance enquiries, and no word came back that in such a hypothetical situation the government would be cross enough to do anything rash. The problem then became one of getting the U.S.-born portion of the Movement to act in an organized way. Working with them was like trying to keep a large litter of puppies cradled in your arms without dropping any or letting any get away. "No, no," I can still remember saying to someone, "*I* can't be the president of the United States! I'm the wrong type for Christ's sake and anyway I don't have *time* to be president of the United States! *You* be the president!" It was hopeless.

My sentiments against the war grew stronger but they grew more intensely private as well. In retrospect I wonder to what extent this was a self-protective device. Here we were, eighteen or twenty years old, being misquoted in *Time*: there was a danger in anti-war celebrity. I remember the sad end of Phil Ochs, the American protest singer, once spoken of in the same sentences with Dylan. He was often in Toronto ("entertaining the troops," he'd say), and wrote at least one of his best-known songs in the tiny dressing room of Bernie Fiedler's Riverboat, one of the dozen or so coffee houses along Yorkville, Cumberland and Avenue Road. We became acquainted. He was a funny, cynical, sharp and gentle man, with an unmistakable voice but a level of musicianship that wasn't thought adequate at the time (but which I heard praised a generation later by a student at one of the best music schools in the United States who was too young to have any interest in the lyrics). I was terribly upset when Ochs hanged himself in his sister's bathroom in New Jersey in 1976, a few months after the war ended. He was troubled by drink and politics, politics and drink: it was difficult to say what the exact relationship was. But surely the timing was not coincidental.

CHAPTER FIVE

LIFE WITHOUT
INSTRUCTION

Elizabeth woods was about ten years older than I was, tall and slender with a strong face and straight dark hair that hung down to her waist. She had been, briefly, one of the volunteers who flitted in and out of the Anansi basement, hoping, I suppose, to have her writing discovered by Dennis Lee. I saw her there only a couple of times and only a few more thereafter, until we bumped into each other at some point early in 1969. She invited me to her small apartment upstairs over a shop on the east side of Church Street between Wellesley and Maitland (almost the entire west side being vacant land in those days, used for overflow parking when the Leafs were performing at Maple Leaf Gardens). This area was not then the centre of gay and lesbian Toronto, as it became some years later, but just a shabby neighbourhood of small 1920s apartment blocks and older run-down houses.

One announced oneself at the apartment—two small bedrooms, a tiny living room, and a kitchen with a dangerously slanting floor—by pulling a string that dangled down from the unenclosed summer porch, activating a small cowbell that hung on a nail upstairs. By rights, the place belonged to an artist named Bill Kimber. He had been sharing it with Eleanor Beattie, an actress, but Liz had grabbed the second bedroom when Eleanor moved on. It had been, I believe, Liz's destiny since adolescence in Prince George, B.C., to preside over some sort of salon, and she had quickly made 489 Church (a different building stands there now) into a sort of all-night drop-in centre for poets and performers and a number of others who approached bohemia from one direction or another without penetrating beyond its raffish fringe. I started spending evenings there myself as part of the crowd, but some of the faces I remember most vividly were those of people who visited only on occasion.

One was Patrick Lane, who had known Liz in high school, and would come by whenever he was in Toronto on poetry business and regale us with stories of logging and hunting and working on fire crews. And it was at 489 Church that I first became aware that Juan Butler, whom I'd known already through the publishers Carol and Peter Martin, was in fact slipping into madness.

Butler, a wildly good-looking guy of mixed Spanish and Irish heritage, had written a short epistolary novel called *Cabbagetown Diary*. It wasn't very important, certainly not worth all the praise it would receive, but it was an accurate forecast of two other far more substantial and more experimental books to come during his all too short career, particularly the anarchist novel *The Garbageman*.

Question: Tell me, in the anarchist society that you envisage, where all men will be free, where no one will ever be in a position to impose his will upon his fellow man, where "doing your own thing" will be the norm rather than the exception, where creative leisure—as opposed to material success—will be the aspired-for work goal, where all political authority will disappear and economic controls will exist on a purely voluntary basis, who will pick up the garbage?

Answer: The garbageman.

I read the manuscript of *Cabbagetown Diary* for Carol and Peter Martin and agreed that they should publish it. At that time, Juan, who was fluent in Spanish, was working as a bartender in some Hispanic restaurant on College Street, and Peter had the idea of throwing a party there to launch the book. As he imagined the scene, all the bigwig reviewers would be there, the Fulfords and the Frenches and so on, being served drinks by this young man in a starched white jacket as they speculated among themselves who—and where—this new genius could be. Just before the suspense became orgasmic, Juan was supposed to leap over the bar, whip off his waiter's tunic and reveal himself as the Author.

Like most of Peter's plans, this one didn't quite work. Invitations were issued, but Juan got fired the day before the event was scheduled to be held. Like me, Juan was forever getting fired, I suppose. Another of his jobs, I remember, was clerking in a bookstore on Yonge Street run by a well-known old Toronto communist.

The proprietor had quit the Party, or at least begun to feel his faith waver, after a doctrinal argument at the communist printing house, during which he had thrown a lead ingot at his antagonist. Now, years later, he was running this bookstore with a full range of hard-to-find political literature of all stripes. He hobbled about on crutches because, it was said, a legal case was still pending that stemmed from an incident in which his ex-wife's bodyguard was alleged to have shot him in the foot. The crutches were necessary, it seemed, because although the wound had healed, the court docket was still very crowded. I would stop in there occasionally, sometimes in the company of Jim Christy (who put out the anarchist paper *Guerrilla* from his tiny apartment over an ultra-expensive jewellery shop on Bloor). The two of us would connive with Juan to ask the proprietor if he had any of the works of, say, Errico Malatesta. We knew what would happen. After first scrutinizing the store and looking up and down Yonge Street to make sure no private investigators were about, he would put down his crutches and, in an almost balletic leap, jump up and grab what we wanted from the very topmost shelf.

Juan, who also wrote some iconoclastic art criticism, lived at this time in a Chinese-run rooming house on Dundonald Street, not far away. In the foyer was a crudely lettered sign imploring the residents in broken English to please flush the communal toilet. When one visited Juan there of an evening to talk about writing, the conversation would be punctuated by an horrendously loud *thwack!* coming from the room immediately above, followed by a light shower of plaster dust from Juan's ceiling. The space overhead was occupied by a man who enjoyed lying abed while trying to kill cockroaches on the opposite wall with a ten-foot bull-whip.

The sad story of Juan Butler is that as his fiction got better and better, his mental state got worse and worse. Such were his vibrations that I once saw a normally quite pacific little dog begin to tear about in irrational circles, crying, barking, cowering, all at the same time, when this human it didn't know approached up the street from a fair distance away. Unlike a number of other people of the sixties, he did manage to make it through the seventies, though barely and with increasing difficulty. One day he appeared with his face tattooed, with *LOVE* spelled backwards under one eye and another word—impossible to make out and probably misspelled—under the other. In 1981, while in psychiatric custody, he hanged himself. He was thirty-seven. Judith Fitzgerald, who I think met him later but knew him much better than I did, published a book of poetry about him.

A much more regular attendant at the Church Street goings-on was Joe Nickell, a slight, good-looking blond chap from Kentucky. He had served in VISTA, the domestic Peace Corps, and had worked on one of the best underground papers, the *Great Speckled Bird* in Atlanta, before fleeing to Canada in his VW van. He was a poet of some talent and sophistication, a former disciple of Wendell Berry, though nothing at all like Berry on the page. Once settled in Toronto, he continued to read and publish poetry and otherwise take his calling seriously. (In my recollection, which is sometimes imperfect, he once

broke a fellow's jaw in an argument about Baudelaire.)
Yet he also developed, as no one else I've ever known has
done, a well-thought-out agenda for the rest of his life. As
a civil servant might say, he established a failure-standard.
That is, he would consider his life a failure unless he
became in turn a professional stage magician, a croupier
in a casino, a stuntman in the movies, a Pinkerton detective—I forget what some of the other goals were. He
accomplished them all. He was also an expert on forgery,
especially as it concerned the chemical properties of various inks and papers.

But in many ways the most appealing character
around Church Street was Bill Kimber, the actual lessee
and a person of immense likability. He was of Ontario
rural stock and had come to the city from St.
Catharines, where he had taken an English degree as
part of the first-ever graduating class at Brock. He had a
large and unusual talent as a visual artist which he was
developing quickly, finding his own style, but he had a
rough go making his way without an art-school background. He was short, quick-witted, hip, verbally playful, always smiling, always flirting with whoever he
met: a person impossible to dislike, a real mensch. But
he had such low self-esteem that he had nicknamed
himself the Gnome. His drawings were of the sort that
people always at a loss when confronted with originality
tended to call Beardsleyesque (for Beardsley was big
then). Gnomes and other such mythical creatures
appeared in them constantly, along with an endless cast
of strong or well-born ladies, ladies of leisure and refine-
ment, all symbols of the unobtainable. He said he
found the Pre-Raphaelites pretty corny, but liked the

spirit in which they were composed. So he had no hesitation about working in figures as seemingly unfashionable as one he called "Irate dumpy wife paying the surprise visit to *la belle dame sans merci* who's stolen her husband's affections." The drawings were obviously a map to what he figured to be his place in the scheme of life. Not for that reason, but because these drawings truly represented an entire imaginative society, they slowly found a loyal audience.

Church Street had only the two bedrooms, but it had a third bed—a narrow camp-bed in one corner of the living room, next to the brick-and-board bookcase—and often at the end of a long evening's wine and conversation I'd simply stay over there, though it was only a few blocks from St. Nicholas. In some past moment of exuberance, someone had jumped on the bed, splintering both of its bottom legs, so that it now more properly resembled a slant-board. I didn't mind. In fact, I liked the people so much that I was considering moving in, as Liz, whose novel was her full-time job, and Bill, who worked with another artist a few nights a week sorting documents at a brokerage house on Bay Street, were having trouble making the rent each month. I had always been happy at St. Nicholas Street, because it had felt like my first real home and the place where I set up shop as a writer. But I was lonely there as well, haunted by what happiness I might have had with Sarah if she hadn't decided, after such long and sometimes painful deliberation, that I fell short of her requirements.

I was talking all this over with Howard Engel one day at the CBC Radio Building, and he pointed out that if I left the loneliness of St. Nicholas Street for the twenty-four-hour bohemian scene on Church Street, I'd have no quiet place to write. So saying, he gave me the key to his office and told me I was free to come in after normal business hours and use it all night if need be, so long as I was gone before the staff started arriving in the morning. I tried to thank him, but he wouldn't let me, telling me instead how Harry Boyle, his own old CBC boss and later a novelist of sorts, once did the same for him, when Howard was just back from Europe, feeling broke and stateless. As space for possessions at Church Street was severely limited, I relived the always painful experience of selling my books to the secondhand bookdealers and moved into what soon proved an even livelier milieu than I had imagined. A somewhat notorious one as well.

Howard was right about the CBC. So long as I was careful not to leave fingerprints that could be found in the morning, I had a splendidly quiet and well-equipped place in which to write, with only a few checks on my concentration. One of these was a Métis named R.R. Sands, a freelance of a kind, who seemed to have copies of *everyone's* keys and who actually *lived* at the CBC. He was a bit of a legend actually. During the day he'd do research (or sleep) in the public library and make the cursory rounds of the *Star Weekly* and the other publications that sometimes bought little squibs of this and that. Other days, he'd put his feet up and watch four old movies in a row at the Biltmore Theatre on Yonge Street. Come nightfall, he would make dinner of the leftovers in the CBC canteen and jiggle the vending machines that sold candy and snacks. He might watch television for a few hours or play music from the immense record library downstairs on one of the office turntables. He kept his changes of clothes, such as they were, in the desk of one of his friends, a producer in the Religion department, who was suspected of being CBC Radio's in-house drug supplier. When necessary, Sands would wash out a few delicate items in the men's loo and have them dry on the radiator before morning. He had staked out the locations of all the sofas in the offices of the more important executives where he might take his well-deserved rest. He even knew that the TV Building across the parking lot had a couple of shower stalls as a convenience for on-air personalities.

Sands was from Olds, Alberta, but seemed rooted in a small bohemian group in Edmonton centred on a few institutions like the club called the Yardbird Suite. I rather liked him, though I found he was uncritically sentimental and almost wept at country music. I used to sometimes get Dan Williman, once his daughters were safely abed, to accompany us to a place in China-town where all the hookers and cabbies hung out (it stayed open until five). But Sands always regarded his stays in Toronto as raiding parties on the great fortified city where all the freelance budgets were kept under guard. When he made a strike by selling some article or (more likely) an idea for a radio programme, he would celebrate wildly. I was with him once when he virtually scaled the face of the parliament buildings at Queen's Park (it was 3:00 a.m. or so) to cut down a huge Maple Leaf flag that he wanted to wear, cloak-like, as a symbol of his victory. When he had enough of a grubstake together, he would return to Edmonton with all his goods in his pack, a Trapper Nelson No. 9, longing for the girlfriend of whom he often spoke (and whose picture he kept in a special pocket sewn into one of his cowboy boots).

Church Street life was unstructured. There were no rules, only the bell on the long cord. The pattern, however, was that anyone could stop by of an evening to read or listen to poetry or argue violently about dialectics, art, whatever. People held their positions tenaciously. Some Marxists from Rochdale were by one night and gave the first long discussions about the women's movement in the city that I remember hearing. More typical, though, were blues jam sessions in the wee hours, often involving excellent musicians. Some guests took enormous liberties, and enormous risks, in bringing their own drugs, not simply marijuana and acid and mescaline (a staple commodity at that time) but worse stuff. What's more, this was at a time when the U.S. Consulate on University Avenue had its hands full making life difficult for dangerous pacifists, and as a number of people who patronized 489 Church were actively in flight from America, this may have helped to bring the place to official notice. The fact that the Church Street scene was freely biracial was probably another sore point with the authorities in a time when Toronto had relatively few people of African descent compared to only a short time later. At least once one of the intelligence-gathering or police agencies made a rather clumsy attempt at infiltration, sending in someone who didn't fit in at all, mainly because he looked as though he had the word *cop* stencilled all over him, from his short-back-and-sides haircut to his shiny shoes. He claimed to be a deserter from Seattle but under gentle questioning could not produce a credible past, including the name of either Seattle newspaper or the call letters of any of its radio stations. One time later, a lone cop in an unmarked car parked for the night in the lot directly across the street, staring intently into our upper porch and occasionally taking notes. Some people were afraid to leave, others no doubt afraid to enter. Once this had gone on for four or five hours, Liz telephoned the Metro cops, playing the distressed woman of the house, explaining how some strange man, probably a rapist or burglar, was watching her apartment. No. 52 Division sent a patrol car. From behind the curtains we could see the pantomime of two cops in low-key professional discourse for a few moments before the Metro one motioned the other (whoever he was) to follow, and they both disappeared. They never tried that particular ploy again.

By June of 1969 it was getting pretty warm on Church Street, unseasonably so, and Liz decided this would be a good time to visit her mother in Vancouver. By diligent application to my clandestine writing on CBC property, I found myself perhaps a thousand dollars ahead of the game. For his part, Bill had sold some drawings, while Liz continued somehow always to exist outside the world of specie. So the three of us decided to slow the metabolism of the apartment and sublet it for the summer. Separately but sometimes together, Bill and I would make our way to the Coast and the three of us would meet at a certain place on a particular day.

Bill was under the mistaken impression that I still had a valid driver's license. I thought he knew that I didn't, as people would sometimes chide me about this, just as they would chide me for not using drugs. Bill found a drive-away agency that would pay him a modest fee to deliver a van to Winnipeg, and he was grumpy the whole time at not having anyone to spell him off on the long trip round the Lakehead. There had been some talk of my doing a poetry reading with Gwen at Winnipeg, but she and I missed each other or the offer was withdrawn, so I decided to push on alone for a time while Bill lingered, seeing artist friends. I hitched rides to Edmonton to see Sands and his strange entourage, which included poets and actors who lived communally in a large old house on the west side. The morning I arrived, they were scattered about from a party the night before, the occasion for which was the arrival of a package from Morocco. It was a fairly straight neighbourhood for such a house, and within the next day or two R.R. and I were refused service at the greasy spoon around the corner because we had long hair (this was a common occurrence in those days, though not usually at obscure greasy spoons). As it happens, a reporter for the Edmonton *Journal* (short-haired) was having a coffee there, saw what happened, interviewed us both, and wrote a story about the city's mistreatment of honest literary fellows.

In a few days Bill turned up, found another free van, this one bound for Vancouver via Calgary. My old Vancouver friends like James Ellis seemed to have vanished in the rain, and so Bill and I started making the rounds of the poets I knew, hoping for someone to put us up overnight. We first called on Seymour Mayne, the poet who had been Pat Lane's partner in publishing the Very Stone House books (an unlikely pairing, I always thought), but he seemed preoccupied, so we went over to bill bissett's place in Kitsilano—a green frame building once occupied by Acorn, I believe, and by a whole exaltation of other poets, stretching back to the dawn of the decade. This was during one of the periods when bill was being shamelessly harassed by the local authorities and may even have been one of the occasions when he was facing some jail time. Certainly he wasn't home, so we entered through a rear window that seemed to invite such egress to the ground floor, a former garage that bill was using as a studio. It was chilly and dank and full of his shamanistic paintings stacked everywhere, warping and mildewing. Our defenestration was as polite and unobtrusive as our entry had been.

Weary now, we began walking round trying to find a room in the West End and finally got something ridiculously cheap in a house on Bute Street, in the first block or so down the hill from Robson. In those days, the characteristic domestic architecture of downtown Vancouver was the wonderful large frame houses with green roof and green trim, of which no more than a handful, I suppose, survived the rush to high-rise apartments and condos that accelerated disgustingly all through the seventies. With his habit of making friends effortlessly (how I envied him his personality), Bill spent half the first night in Vancouver talking with a sixty-year-old merchant sailor who lived across the hall and liked to drink a lot and misquote Shelley, which he did proudly and from memory. When someone banged on the door the following morning, I naturally feared that the seafarin' man was back. To my surprise, the caller was John Newlove, one of the poets I and everybody else, it seemed, most admired. Such was the speed of the bush telegraph that he knew of our arrival almost before we'd unpacked. He'd changed greatly since I'd seen him last in Toronto, where he worked at McClelland & Stewart. Some bladder ailment had made his him swell up alarmingly, and he'd gone completely grey.

I spent the summer running into poets and writers I knew and meeting other ones for the first time. Through a reading, I got to know Stanley Cooperman, who had written an interesting study of the American novel in the First World War and created a poetic alter ego for himself in a character named Cappelbaum, who, like Cooperman, seemed to toss off poems with an easy fluency bordering on glibness. Cooperman had taught at Indiana and a number of other American universities. For a while, he had even taught in Iran, during the heyday of the Pahlavi dynasty; as a sideline, he wrote for the English-language paper, doing a night-club column headed "Teheran after Dark."

He was a man who worked hard at being unusual. One example was his obsession with owls. Owls riddled his books, such as his selected poems, *The Owl behind the Door*, and he and Jennifer's house in North Van was infested with stuffed owls, paintings of owls, plastic owls, wooden owls—hundreds of owl images in all. Cooperman was disliked at Simon Fraser and beyond, because he was part of the vast in-migration of American academics that took over English departments across the country during this time. He never seemed to fit into Canada very well, but I mean this as a compliment as well as a criticism, for neither did he seem to fit in within the army of occupation of which he was part.

He was a profoundly unhappy man, I thought, with a strong vein of displaced irony. He killed himself in his Simon Fraser office not long afterwards, in 1974, and was almost instantly forgotten as a poet. One prominent and perpetually angry figure on the Vancouver scene wrote that Cooperman was "an unattractive man who is remembered only by those who didn't like him." It's to contradict that statement and protest that kind of brutality that I write of him here.

One day when I was out with Bill I bumped into Avo Erisleau (one of the original contributors to *Tish*, though no longer called to mind as such); he had been working at the Ryerson Press in Toronto before its controversial closure, and was now off to Tanzania as a CUSO volunteer. The last Bill and I saw of him was this thin blond Scandinavian figure using his copy of *Teach Yourself Swahili* to wave goodbye to us from the window of the train. Jim Brown of Talonbooks took me round to see Warren Tallman (the only time I've ever met him); we sat in his back garden while the Tallman family dog raced round and round a tree without stopping, and I met up again with Phyllis Webb, who had quit the CBC and returned to her native province: we had a picnic on the beach.

Earle Birney was especially attentive and friendly and kept inviting me to call on him at his high-rise apartment on Barclay Street near English Bay (which high-rises in too great abundance had not then obscured from view). He was still trying to edit a complete annotated edition of the poetry of his late friend Malcolm Lowry in partnership with Lowry's widow, Marjorie, and the collaboration was proving difficult (the book, as such, never got published). To raise his spirits, Earle was composing poems on Japanese paper, which he would make into elaborate kites and release over the beach, hoping the air currents might actually carry one to some culture beyond our own. He was already of retirement age but was still aggressively in pursuit of, not the past (which he avoided talking about), but youth. He kept rewriting and rewriting his poems, and republishing and republishing them, making them younger and younger looking on the page, while his new work at this time was an enthusiastic embrace (never quite successful, I thought) of the op, the pop and the concrete. He was still living with his first wife, Esther, who would sometimes appear in the apartment when I was there, once saying out loud, and with total lack of conviction, how lucky she felt to be living among books and manuscripts.

One July day, Earle was showing me something while the television blared in the corner of the living room. It was the live transmission of the first human landing on the Moon.

"This is a historic occasion," I said. "A milestone in the life of imperial America. A generation from now, people will remember where they were and what they were doing."

"Don't be an ass," Earle said. "This is hype, nothing more, engineered by the Americans for public-relations purposes and of no lasting interest whatever to anybody else."

We were both right.

Bill was slightly peeved when I got back.

"You left at six in the morning saying you were making a phone call and then I didn't see you all evening. You're always doing that."

But we fell quite naturally into a rhythm that summer that was highly productive for us both and, given the cramped quarters, this was no mean achievement.

He would rise early and hit the beach, inspired to work by the lithe bodies all around him, or else, if it were raining, go body-hunting through the West End. At City Hall one day he met Vancouver's official town fool, Joachim Foikis, and came back rhapsodizing about his beauty of movement, his jester suit and his beatific face. Bill was working alternately in his dreamworld mode and in another more darkly surreal vein.

"The universe is perverse," he would say on these latter occasions. "Therefore I would like to illustrate it with sacred normalcies."

When the light waned, he would trudge back to Bute Street where I would often still not be awake and so would sometimes be his sleeping model unwittingly. "You're an interesting sleeper," he said to me once as I woke to find him with the chair drawn up next to the bed, scratching away in his sketch book. "You slept in several new positions today. For comic relief, I liked the one where you wrapped yourself up in the sheets like a cocoon and sort of wore the pillow on your head like a turban."

We'd cook our rude meal together (once stinking up the whole house so badly with tainted fish that we had to evacuate for twenty-four hours). Or else we would eat for a buck or two at the Doors in Chinatown and kick round down in skid row way out East Hastings, where there was a Yonge Street type of movie house we liked—the Lux. Then it would be Bill's turn to assume the single bed. I'd mould my long legs into the spring-busted easy chair with the 1940s upholstery and begin my night's writing. Sometimes he'd snore all night long, which I found restful. At one time, a sound-truck would slowly crawl up and down the streets of the rooming house district, broadcasting its never-changing message: "Fifty lovely girls who wanna meet you tonight down at the Marco Polo. Yessir, fifty lovely girls."

Towards the end of the summer, Sands decided to hitch over the mountains to join the three of us (for Liz had turned up by then and was briefly sharing a hotel room her mother was paying for). But finances were running low. As I had the most, I lingered the longest, I guess, and finally hitched back to Toronto in two great arcs—Vancouver to Winnipeg non-stop and Winnipeg to Toronto. Bill had a theory that hitchhiking eastward was always easier than hitching westward, an experience that notoriously becalmed people for days in places like Wawa.

"It's the trade winds," he would say.

I've known no other artist who sketched as constantly as Bill did. There was never a moment, such as when Liz was in the bathtub reading Peter Beagle, one of her favourite writers, when he wasn't likely to appear with a Rapidograph and one of his sketch-books bound in black pebbled cloth. I think he was around too many writers and musicians and not enough other visual artists. Mind you, I think he found these associations useful in a number of ways. Once I brought Margaret Atwood over to see his stuff, which, with her love of the Gothic, she liked at once, as I knew she would. She bought a number of drawings, sent Bill off to the studio of her friend Charlie Pachter and, most importantly of all, got him to do the famous tarot card cover design for her collection *Power Politics* a couple of years later. There was a lot of technique freely exchanged in those days. Joe Nickell, who in one of his careers had been a travelling sign-painter and in another a political cartoonist, introduced Bill to coloured inks. Bill in turn first got Pat Lane interested in drawing, which has remained a part of his poetry, and even gave him one of his Rapidographs. Writers were Bill's fans and his patrons. One year I paid him to design book plates for me and some of my book collecting friends, and this led to other small commissions from outside the circle. Paul Martin, the Liberal senator, saw one of them and extended a commission of his own. At this time Bill was also managing to sell some spot drawings to *Quarry*, the *Fiddlehead* and other literary magazines, and some cover illustrations for small presses. His finest job as a book artist was one he hated, doing six large illustrations for *Black Azure*, a book of poetry by Walter (Bud) Osborn in an edition of 250 copies. The author was one of the numberless young writers who passed in and out of 489. I can recall nothing of him except that he was always seen in the company of a fellow called Shelley who seldom spoke or bathed.

Bill was playing with juxtaposing visual references in these drawings, using both Rapidograph and a brush, pulling back a lot on his symbolist vocabulary in favour of something more like the brand of German expressionism that surfaced, transmuted, in the U.S. during the 1920s, in people like Wallace Smith. The six *Black Azure* illustrations were all figures, ones that resembled the artist. The most impressive was a drawing of a couple locked in coital embrace. The man, on top, with his back and bum to the viewer, had Bill's body, while the woman on the bottom, looking up from the centre of a great sunburst of hair, had Bill's face.

So while these writerly connections were good for him, I felt he suffered from want of contact with other visual artists. His one artist-friend was Michael Behnan who was often part of the crowd along with his wife, Sue, and there were sketching sessions and general shop talk. (Behnan later went in a very different direction artistically, towards a kind of folk art, and had a meteoric vogue in the commercial galleries and with important critics; he died of cancer in the 1980s when he was only thirty-five.)

Bill only began to participate in a visual art scene when he got laid off from his menial part-time job in the Bay Street counting house. He was always sorely pressed for money (unlike Liz, who had no money but never seemed to let it bother her). Student loans lay heavily on his conscience, and now he would be locked in a long combat with the unemployment insurance authorities as well. He decided he should throw himself into being a life model at different art schools around the city. No one ever applied himself to the task with more dedication, both in learning to be a good model in the way that each situation demanded and in beating on doors to drum up work; he would come home moaning, "A rough day in the naked business." Eventually, he was working variously at the U of T, York, the Artists' Studio, the New School, the public school system, even at a seniors' home. He often modelled for classes instructed by people as established as—to take three very different examples—Dennis Burton, known for his grossly erotic paintings of women in garter belts; Telford Fenton, known for his portraits and theatrical scenes; and Kenneth Lochheed, one of the original Regina Five, who must have been some sort of visiting teacher in Toronto round this time. At length, Bill became one of the most trusted models, with the skill and discipline to form a specialty in what was called Life without Instruction: classes with a model but no teacher to give orders or criticize. In time Bill even acquired some private clients, including one man who had him travel to his suburban home to be photographed as Nude Christ in Chains.

What strikes me as most curious now as I look back is how people managed to get their creative work done given the fact that there were wild parties in those days—wild. A note survives in my memory about someone called Electric Martha, who would always offer acid to whoever wanted some, in contradistinction to those people whose drug of choice was a compound called MDA. The drug stuff always made me uneasy. Big Bill Lias was right in that respect: it was nothing but trouble. What made the parties so unusual, though, was their extreme breadth. A lot of people of the older generation would turn up, as when Al Purdy or someone like that would be in Toronto giving a reading and would stop by and stay all hours, as a party sort of welled up around him. The same almost happened once with Allen Ginsberg, I remember, who was reading in the area, but I couldn't get him to follow me back to Church Street.

Sometimes things got a little rowdy. Peter Martin, the perpetually struggling publisher, a drink in one hand, made some extravagant claim with the other, putting his arm through the glass in the kitchen window and cutting himself up to the elbow. Another time I fell—tumbled actually, in an inebriated ball—down the flight of thirty or so stairs leading to the street, and it pains me to remember that I once poured a beer on the head of Paddy Hynan, an expatriate Irish fellow who did literary documentaries for CBC Radio. He was one of Liz's many male friends. I forget what obnoxious thing he had said, but it must have been more obnoxious than my response. Once a six-piece band arrived and announced they would play all night. They were still at it at three, at four, at five. Poor Bill would sometimes return from a modelling job at night to find his bed occupied by multiple strangers. Or else he would have a few hours to recuperate between the end of a party and the beginning of a tiring commute to a life-drawing class at some remote outpost of culture such as the Scarborough campus of the U of T or even Sheridan College. Other mornings, though, he would be free, and there was always something invigorating, after being up all night, about walking with him down Yonge Street just after dawn when the air was still clean and crisp in our lungs and we were still young enough to be proud of how we could abuse our bodies with delayed retribution we mistook for impunity.

The parties, the talk, the drink, the smoke, the marathon work sessions, the essentially manic nature of everything we did was, I think now, consistent with a lot of young people who somehow resented the youth which they were supposed to relish, and were eager to accrue experience at far faster than the normal human rate. In doing so, we sacrificed a lot of intimacy for the sake of sex and missed a lot of chances at friendship in the welter of acquaintance. We were a noisy community of strangers.

Looking at my work from those days, and at Bill's, I know that he saw this more clearly than I did.

"I did a drawing today of a monk gazing out his cell window," he said once over breakfast at the Devon, a nearby Chinese restaurant we frequented.

"Sounds William Morrisy."

He paid no attention.

"There's an unfinished illuminated manuscript on the writing table. I'm feeling very monkish lately. I really think I understand their way of life."

He was serious.

"In Anglo-Saxon days monks were often lonely men who entered the monastery because it was the only place that would accept strangers. They'd often been strangers or outcasts from the small family-kingdoms. Strangers were unwelcome: once you separated from your family, you were *really* alone. I feel like that sometimes. Forced to accept a solitary life, separated from the good times and the women. Living through others and through the imagination…." He trailed off, taking the Chinese teacup in both hands. "The detail work," he said.

Men were always calling on Liz, in what seemed to me an almost old-fashioned kind of way. I don't mean without lustful intent when appropriate but in some manner that befit her role as the penniless patroness who ran a salon whose fame, or notoriety, was spreading. One night she had dinner with Stephen Vizinczey, whom I believe she met through George Jonas, his compatriot in the Hungarian Revolution. She mentioned at dinner that Bill had been doing some erotic drawings—that is to say, drawings whose eroticism was more in the open than customary. There was one in particular which Bill described as "masseuse deciding to give an evil client a hand job." Vizinczey was most eager to see the portfolio. Bill should be "discovered," he said. He promised to use his influence with an important critic in England (who was it? Edward Lucie-Smith perhaps? I forget) to have a book of his erotic work published there. People were always saying such things to him. In time, he learned not to get his hopes up.

Another of Liz's friends was Don Cullen. In fact, Don was everyone's friend. He was an actor and comedian who back in the late 1950s had founded a coffee house called the Bohemian Embassy, a famous establishment while it lasted. I used to pass its boarded-up entrance every day on my way from the bottom of St. Nicholas Street heading north. The young Dylan had played there, the young Peggy Atwood had given her first reading there. Gwen, too, had been a regular, and there were close and intricate ties between it and the Gerrard Street Village. Don was forever looking for some opportunity to reopen the place in a new location, and eventually did so, first at Rochdale and then, years later, on Queen Street. It was the literary reading series he launched at the Rochdale venue that eventually grew into the Harbourfront readings and literary festivals that became so much a part of Toronto's cultural life in the 1980s and 1990s.

Don was a fine fellow with good taste (he later married Janet Inksetter, who later married me and then set herself up as an antiquarian bookseller), but I think he failed to see that the coffee house era, developed round acoustic music, was pretty much gone. There were still some dreary poetry readings at the Penny Farthing on Yorkville and acts still played at the Riverboat down the street, the other survivor from the old era, but already, in just eighteen months or so, Yorkville had changed radically, with expensive boutiques forcing out the coffee bars and head shops. But all Don's talk about the Embassy, I believe, had put it in Liz's head to open a sort of small updated version of the coffee house ideal, as an extension of the scene at Church Street, or perhaps as a way to impose some order on it. An inspiration of a different kind may have been John Robert Colombo. In those days, before retreating from the literary scene for a career in pop trivia and research into the paranormal, John liked to be at the centre of things, in perhaps what he fancied was the manner of some ersatz European *littérateur*, and he started a series of fortnightly get-togethers, where book-industry people and artsy folks would mill about, drinking and talking. John was ill-advised enough to christen this enterprise the Family Compact: not everyone was certain that he intended the name ironically. The most interesting aspect of these soirées was the location. They were held in the cellar of the

Temple Building, the wonderful Romanesque sky-scraper which Oronhyatekha, the wealthy Mohawk businessman, had erected in the 1890s on the southwest corner of Queen and Bay, kitty-corner to the Old City Hall, whose style it complemented. The building was callously pulled down shortly thereafter to make way for the ugly world headquarters of Thomson Newspapers, and Colombo's band never regrouped.

So it was, in any event, that Liz and a core of perhaps a dozen Church Streeters operated a place called the Soft Cell in a third floor industrial space down on King between Church and Yonge, and on regularly pre-scribed evenings would organize readings and perfor-mances there, and made plans for an accompanying magazine, to be called *Bread*, taking its name from the elusive substance sought by all.

The other extension of Church Street was a farm in Renfrew County, in eastern Ontario, which had come into the possession of Al and Eurithe Purdy through inheritance from Eurithe's side of the family. It was not much of a farm—twenty-five acres of more or less until-lable land with the usual old frame farmhouse that the wind whistled through—and yet it was lovely, set on the face of a small hill with woods behind and an enor-mous barn that Bill instantly dismissed as Wyethesque. Al and Eurithe were getting no use out of it and so kindly offered to lease it to me for only $600 a year, which I figured I could just barely afford. I planned to use the place to get away to from time to time when I had to make headway on some more substantial piece of writing. In fact, the others, perhaps as many as a dozen at a time, used it more than I did. Joe Nickell, the poet and polymath cursed with ownership of a van, was charged with transporting everyone and enough supplies for all. The size of the load combined with the condition of the van meant that the trip sometimes took six hours though the distance was only about 150 miles. One day, when all was peaceful, Eurithe stopped by to visit, bringing Margaret Laurence, who lived near Peterborough. I was glad they didn't see the place at its more typical. There was also a lot of sexual activity taking place—ménages divisible by factors of two and three. Some people seemed to sign on for weekends in that expectation—with Liz and Joe benefiting the most, if envy has not clouded my recollection. Also, those who dropped acid did so regularly there, and either lay down for long reposes or else cavorted merrily through the woods and across the meadow and round the pond that was home to two beavers. My private view was that this was much safer than their tripping-out in the city, especially if the buddy system were strictly enforced.

I was in the habit of spending Thursday evenings in the back room of the Village Book Store on Gerrard Street West. This was the establishment of Marty Ahvenus, the person who by talking me up to Howard Engel had helped me land my job at the CBC. Marty is a wonderful man to whom I was first introduced by Raymond Souster, the poet who spent his weekdays in the securities department in the cellar of the Canadian Imperial Bank of Commerce's main branch. Marty was the friend of all writers and artists and small-press publishers. He had grown up in Toronto's now totally forgotten Finnish community whose centre of gravity was near Dundas and Beverley Streets, and being blessed with a likeable manner and a taste for conversation he had first been a travelling salesman and had also worked the front desk in hotels. But he knew he wanted to be a bookseller—he was already a part-time book scout—and so he threw over secure employment and took a lease on the tiny two-storey building on Gerrard, formerly a Chinese fraternal lodge. He lived upstairs, sold books out of the front part of the ground floor, and on Thursday evenings convened these parties in the smaller room behind.

These were opportunities for Marty to reminisce. Sometimes he would tell us about the great meals he had had at the most out-of-the-way little places in his days on the road. Though many years had gone by, he could still rhapsodize about the pecan pie at a diner outside Saskatoon, for example. But mostly the talk was about books and the book trade. Marty himself had marked but unusual tastes in his personal reading. He was particularly fond of Jack Kerouac's *Dr. Sax*, giving away dozens of copies in an attempt to make converts, and when Kerouac died in October 1969, he draped the shop window and made a little memorial display of Kerouac's works. He also liked cookery books, books about the hotel business and the writings of the Czech fantasist Karel Čapek (who coined the term *robot*). The other regulars at Marty's Thursdays included an Irish playwright, a former clergyman turned dealer in Canadian art and assorted other booksellers and collectors—and one librarian, our friend Richard Landon, of the U of T rare books department. From time to time Marty would gather those still ambulatory after these sessions and take us out for a substantial meal.

It was while returning worse for the wear from one of these that I first met, and heard, Jim Byrnes, "Missouri Jim" as he tried to call himself for a while. There was no deception involved. A ruggedly handsome guy with thick straight black hair and an unbeatably diabolical smile, Jim was a blues singer of transcendent talent (his version of "Guns and Roses" was a magnificent affair) and was in fact a native Missourian. He was also, at that moment, on the lam from the U.S. Army at Fort Leavenworth, Kansas, after a bizarre series of incidents, adventures and hair's-breadth escapes which he retold to entertain those who chose to listen only to their narrative surface. Bill characterized him at once as a "priceless madman." Liz and I were instantly drawn to him, too, each in our different way, but then everybody liked Jim. He had a voice with a bit of whisky in it and was linguistically very playful while, at the same time, projecting a faint suggestion of danger, perhaps somewhat as Byron is said to have done. One day Mike Behnan was cutting Bill's hair in the kitchen and I overheard the two of them discussing how individuals like Jim seemed to have bigger adrenalin glands than other people.

"I wonder what I'd be like if I ever actually snapped?" Bill said.

"You'd be catatonic," Mike replied. "I'd be violent."

"No, I'd rather be violent. I mean, isn't the whole point to suddenly wig out and become totally unlike your old self?"

In any event, no one of us had any doubt in our minds that Jim was destined for musical stardom. Certainly it took him no time whatever to be the biggest draw in every non-union room in downtown Toronto. At some point quite early on, he went from being a single to being part of a duo. His partner, escaping not the military but America and God knows what else, was an almost equally memorable musician, though without the same stage magic.

This was because he was frequently incoherent from heroin: here was a drug problem on a level I didn't much care to contemplate. I'll call him Phillip, though I suspect that he's been beyond hearing for some years now, dead or in prison.

———

In January 1970 Liz would be turning thirty—it seemed impossible, she looked so young—and we, the standing committee of disconsolate bohemians who were her friends, decided to throw her a party. No, a wake, to mourn the death of her youth. After a good deal of nagging, we had persuaded the landlord of the building, who ran a pizza joint on Yonge Street, to enclose the long verandah or rather to give us enough extra-heavy PVC to do so ourselves. (He did, but he also hiked the rent, to $181 a month, and our relations with him were never the same after that.) This extra space wasn't heated but could be warmed by cramming enough bodies into it. We would invite everyone any of us knew and announce it as a masquerade. It was going to be a strange affair.

By this time a couple of the people who routinely spent the pre-dawn hours at Church Street had found themselves renting accommodations across town at the lower end of Beverley Street, where there was a once-magnificent terrace of white 1880s houses with mansard roofs: places now preserved with pride but then in a poor state of repair indeed and subject to rumours about their demolition. Some of the planning took place there as well, which drew other people in the process. Some of these were transvestite friends of friends, who set about helping with costumes in a few cases. For example, they made Bill a pierrot costume. "For some reason," he said earnestly, "it makes me look like an East Indian drag queen in desert boots, none of which I am." Later, he found he had to wear it with silk pajama bottoms to really make it work for him.

It was only at this point that male homosexuals (the word *gay* was just beginning to become current in this context, struggling against the neologism *homophile*, which soon lost out) were becoming conspicuous in the arts world in Toronto. Liz and Bill and many others would always make a production of Hallowe'en when the transvestites left the safety of the St. Charles Tavern, a converted Victorian fire hall on Yonge Street with a decaying clock-tower, and took to parading up and down outside—the one night of the year they could do so without the threat of police harassment, according to an unwritten code. Later, thinking back on my friend Bill, I wonder what his private thoughts were. Foolish of me, but I never knew; it was an area we never touched on. Anyway, looking at his work, and enjoying his personality, you could see that while he was the farthest thing imaginable from a misogynist he nonetheless always positioned himself in the role of someone whom the women he knew and drew would always reject. This was not an anthropological phenomenon, like something out of *The White Goddess*. Here was a person we cared about deeply, and often shared a platonic bed with, beginning to enter some great period of doubt and torment that you couldn't help but recognize in his work but that we, I, couldn't see clearly enough in his life to help with in any way that would matter. "I've done a drawing of a drunken gnome in heat, pestering party-ladies," he said in anticipation of the forthcoming masque. "I guess I have a rather sickeningly good-natured view of my own absurdity." He laughed.

I must say it was a memorable wake. The press thought so and so, I believe, did the police. The place was thronged with an incredibly wide cross-section of people. Some, such as Stephen Mezei, were quite imaginative in their get-ups. He was another of those urbane Hungarians who had fled first the Nazis and then the communists. Now he was the editor of *Performing Arts in Canada*, the sort of perpetually penniless magazine for which we, Liz and I, both wrote, and Bill drew. Stephen came as a mad Turk, with pantaloons, a brocade waistcoat covering his hairy chest, and a red tarboosh. His wife, Rosa, whose English was less perfect than his, wore an antique gold-threaded cape and told everyone she was supposed to be an imp.

On climbing the long narrow stairs, the guests were overpowered by the smell of funeral incense, only to be met by me, the usher, in my frock coat, who showed them (*ushered* them, I suppose I should say) to the verandah. There lay Liz, stretched out in a black coffin. It had been built by one of the hangers-on, Ken

Williams, and painted by Liz herself, who had lined it in white satin. Ruthie Nickell, Joe's wife (for only a short time longer), struck a series of convincingly grief-stricken poses and wailed like the best-paid mourner imaginable, except that she was doing so for free. The crowd was belly-to-belly and hip-to-hip and included, I remember, one young man in what looked like his grandmother's see-through flapper dress. He was a friend of Sandy Stagg, a person most of us met that night for the first time, who would turn out to be the animating force in what lay ahead for Toronto bohemia and one of the important characters in the social history of the city. In the morning, the bodies of those who couldn't make it home lay scattered throughout the apartment in undignified postures of slumber. Bill's mattress was soaking wet, we couldn't tell why. There was broken glass and bits of food everywhere, and extraneous bits of costumes that had come loose or been jettisoned during the festivities.

———

I had scarcely started working for Anansi when I became acquainted with Peggy Atwood. One side of her family had long, thick roots in Nova Scotia, and though not reared there herself, she had a bit of the Maritimes twang in her voice. It was a remarkable voice, once heard never forgotten, full of unexpected inflections, but one which tended towards a monotone when she read poetry in public. That's what she was doing when I first encountered her. We were in Victoria College. She was standing behind a lectern that was too tall for her, reading *The Circle Game* and some of her forthcoming work, *The Animals in That Country*, into a superfluous microphone. I sat at the back of the room, ready to sell copies of the former text from a folding card table.

Sometimes it seemed she had been at the University of Toronto with about half of the individuals I was coming into contact with in my professional dealings: the magazine editors, publishing people and other writers who were all starting to get their first really important jobs now that they were in their early thirties. Peggy was loyal to all of them and they to her. She had many impressive qualities, including a level of justified self-confidence I had never encountered before (her parents must have loved her from the instant of birth), but I think loyalty was the most attractive of her many attributes. It was the rarest and the one people would most like having themselves. When Peggy was your friend, she was your friend for life (and what's more, in a world of impractical poets and artists, she was worldly-wise in the extreme). With people who didn't quite qualify as contemporaries, she had a special kind of almost sisterly relationship, and that certainly applied to some of the folks at Church Street, particularly Bill, whose work she continued to buy while trying to find others who would do the same. She was really good that way.

Because her reputation and talent made her the senior person in any group in which I could claim even probationary status, I was always fascinated to see not only her easily jocular relationship with her contemporaries like Dennis Lee, but also how she acted with those of the older generation whose work or pioneering accomplishments she admired. There was some note of uneasy deference in her long (but never particularly intense) acquaintanceship with Earle Birney or Al Purdy (but definitely not Irving Layton, whose braggadocio and ballyhoo could only irritate her). It was in this connection that I recall a trip to Montreal a couple of weeks after Liz's wake.

Some congress of poets was taking place—possibly under the auspices of the new League of Canadian Poets, I'm not certain—and the Montreal locals such as Louis Dudek, Frank Scott and the now almost forgotten Ron Everson were the hosts of one or another of a string of small parties. I admired Dudek as a humanist but found him dour as a personality, not to say sour, while I fear he must have seen me as a speechless barbarian. Certainly he gave me the impression of someone who, having risen from the stigma of an immigrant neighbourhood to study at Columbia, befriend Pound and return to McGill in a triumph of respectability, could not now help but look down on an immigrant who had done none of those things. As for Scott, he was a lesser poet (and, as events during the October Crisis a few months distant were about to prove, a great lifelong champion of civil liberties except when they were most in danger). But he was a certified Great Canadian. It was my privilege during this period to meet a number of that breed. They always gave me a satisfying chill of historical recognition, the same feeling I had the time John Diefenbaker threatened to sue me (a rather common distinction but one I cherish). Scott, an impressive figure with kind eyes and a profile befitting the notarial class, told the story of a 1964 canoe trip with Pierre

Trudeau and a number of other male friends in the Northwest Territories. Scott had been taking 8mm film of the trip and had captured Trudeau clowning in the nude after a ritual morning swim in the river. The instant Trudeau became prime minister, Scott said, Mounties appeared at his door and confiscated the film. (Scott later revised the story to the form given in Sandra Dwja's biography of him, in which Scott does the gentlemanly thing, calling the Mounties' attention to the existence of the film and voluntarily submitting it for destruction lest it fall into the wrong hands.)

Peggy said that she wanted me to meet a friend of hers, John Glassco, known as Buffy. Domestically, his standing as a poet, a rather conventional type of poet, was in recession at that point, while his international reputation as a pornographer had yet to become widely known here. I knew the name mainly because I had just finished reading a wonderful excerpt from his forthcoming book, *Memoirs of Montparnasse*, in the *Tamarack Review*. It told of his being bounced out of a party at the studio of Gertrude Stein ("a large rhomboidal woman"). Later, of course, it became known that *Memoirs of Montparnasse* was not what it claimed to be, a work begun on the spot in Paris in 1928 and finished back in Canada in 1931, but a work mostly of the 1960s—and largely of the imagination. He did not, for example, know the old roué Frank Harris, as he would claim.

Glassco had come from a modestly wealthy family, but had spent much of his adult life separated from them, living simply in the Eastern Townships, writing poetry and delivering the Royal Mail for a livelihood.

These days he was keeping a place in Montreal, a basement apartment on the west side of Mountain Street, if I recall correctly. This seemed perfect: it was as inexpensively as one could live and still be round the corner from the Ritz.

Peggy had made an appointment for us to see him at ten in the morning. When we arrived, he affected not to be expecting us, but he was wearing a silk smoking-jacket and a cravat and was having his breakfast champagne. Perhaps because he had heard that I took a liking to them (chameleons are the most polite of creatures), he made a point of playing up the colonial aristo, posing, with perhaps a bit more enthusiasm than strict accuracy allowed, as a sort of dissolute and bohemian Vincent Massey. I told him how much I had enjoyed the chapter in the *Tamarack* and asked when the book itself might appear and (obvious question) whether he had known the other famous expats of 1920s Paris— Joyce or the Fitzgeralds perhaps or Hemingway? "Ah, Hemingway," he replied. "Big, rambunctious American sort of chap, you know. Always eating bacon and eggs, as I remember him. Most curious." He furrowed his brow in distaste at the recollection.

Peggy's admiration for Buffy as a mischief-maker as well as an artist was palpable and obvious, respectively. Later, when we had joined him in champagne and strawberries, he took an ornate little lock from the pocket of his smoking-jacket and opened the front of an antique *cloisonné* secretary to retrieve a book.

"Douglas, perhaps you might be interested in seeing my latest work."

It was called *The Temple of Pederasty* and purported

to be the translation, by a modern Japanese, of an ancient Japanese text by one Ihara Saikaku. But of course this was an honourable and expedient tradition, born of long years of persecution, thinly disguising the fact that the entire text was a John Glassco production from first to last. Later, he took down a copy of the Grove Press edition of Aubrey Beardsley's unfinished pornographic novel *Under the Hill* and pointed out the exact spot where the original manuscript ended and he, Buffy, had picked up the thread and finished the story in faultless imitation of Bearsdley's style.

But it was *The Temple of Pederasty* that was on his mind. Later that night he and Peggy and I and George and Angela Bowering had dinner together at some unprepossessing Chinese restaurant in the East End that was supposed to be renowned for its fish. Buffy fantasized that public demand would soon make a second printing of *The Temple* necessary and that, to satisfy this eventuality, we should all compose jacket blurbs. He passed a pen and blank sheet of paper round the table. George wrote in praise of the subject matter, saying that if his mother had taken him to a pederast when he was a boy he wouldn't have bad feet today. When the paper came to me I wrote, "John Glassco's *The Temple of Pederasty* is a book that leaves nothing to be desired." But Peggy produced a splendidly subtle squib, a thing so expert that only physical examination could have detected the tip of her tongue in her cheek.

When I got back to Toronto quite late the next evening, Bill told me that the plans for a bunch of people to go to the farm had taken an unexpected turn. Someone (not Joe Nickell but a new recruit) was going to drive them there "but he seems to be in a bit of a predicament. He's gone mad. No, really. He's having wild, interesting adventures which could lead to his arrest and deportation." Certainly they were enough to postpone the trip and leave the living room, hallway, perhaps even the kitchen of No. 489, studded with sleeping bodies. On my own broken-down bed, no wider than a seaman's bunk, there were two poets who hated each other when awake. Not for the first time, I accepted Bill's invitation to share his room for the night. As always, he was a perfect gentleman, because he had not yet come to terms with being otherwise. What's more, it was so cold all through the house that everyone could only sleep wearing multiple layers of clothing, including sweaters. Even then, we shivered.

———

There were troubles in Bohemia. Phillip, the other blues guitarist who worked with Jim Byrnes, was squeezing a friend of Liz's named Mary-Anne Carpentier, a Franco-ontarien from Sudbury or Timmins who had moved south to study art conservation. Phillip had come to expect that she would help satisfy his heroin habit.

She claimed that when she failed or refused to do so, he beat her. This was starting to feel like being back in A———. I didn't like using the word anymore, or hearing it.

The positive note was Sandy Stagg, the very smart blonde Cockney who, second only to the corpse of hon-our, had been the big hit of Liz's wake. Originally, she had come to Canada attached to a thoroughly anglicized, Canadian-born male journalist who eventually returned to England without her. This was London's loss. Sandy was a vibrant spirit who made lots of creative activity happen by working at it or simply by standing still and letting others spin off from her own enthusiasm. Her disciplines were all decorative ones, her talent was a talent for making shifts in taste. At the moment she had found an empty theatre somewhere down by Soho Street and saw it as a great umbrella for various groups. She dragged Liz and others along to see it, thinking that the Soft Cell might move there. The energy had been leaking out of the Cell pretty fast, particularly since the night a freak blizzard kept everyone at home and the person who was supposed to be reading—Dennis Lee—was in bed with the 'flu. Sandy thought the Cell could revitalize itself as one of the client elements of this old theatre, which she also visualized as harbouring everyone from renegade fashion designers to erotic conceptual artists.

After protracted dreaming and negotiations, nothing came of that particular idea, but a lot more was to come from Sandy. She was one of the people somehow connected to the start of the Open Studio. At the time the Studio was pretty much the only alternative business of any sort on Queen Street West, which was then a run-down section of the city, with the usual greasy restaurants, beer parlours and specialized industrial-supply shops. It was a working-class streetscape, with the windows of all the crumbling Victorian buildings blacked out on the second and third storeys and with the tan-and-purple streetcars rattling along out front, picking up dreary people here and depositing other dreary people there. Later, after the period covered in these notes, she took over one of the old restaurants, the Peter Pan, and made it the focal point of the reinvention of Queen Street as the main drag of artistic Toronto. At least one other restaurant followed, and an antique-clothing business that caught people's fancy at just the right time. She was one of the great visionaries of Toronto culture, one of the main custodians of the city's artistic self. You never knew what she was working on. One day she stopped by struggling under the weight of two enormous parcels, the one of pork chops, the other of artificial fur. Whatever she started was soon copied by dozens of other people, and some area was brought back to life, a different kind of life. Later she worked her magic in London, where she had to return regularly to supply her shops, and in New York. She threw terrific parties, much better than ours: more original, certainly more colourful. By April there was talk of Sandy moving into a larger house down near Queen where more people could be accommodated. This was followed by talk of our giving up Church Street so as to be sufficiently near by that the two scenes could really merge. The tectonic plates under Bohemia were shifting.

Jim and Phillip were playing everywhere together and never to less than enthusiastic if not always coherent audiences. Their biggest venue was the Global Village at 17 St. Nicholas, a combination espresso place and theatre, with red, green and black lights and seating on various levels, where the wildness might just be getting started at 1:00 a.m. or so. Mary-Anne had got out of her abusive relationship with Phillip, thank God, but he was cutting a swath through the rest of the population and also, we suspected, feeding his habit by other means—namely, threatening and robbing terrified Korean immigrant families who ran milk stores. We had no direct proof of this. But it got so that his haunts, including ours, were being watched again, and once, when two of our acquaintances were crossing the border at Fort Erie, they were stopped and interrogated for a couple of hours about Phillip, his movements, his aliases, his whereabouts, the other people he knew. Suffice it to say his reputation had begun to precede him wherever he went. But I can't remember to what extent, if at all, this was a factor in the three of us deciding to give notice to the landlord and move somewhere closer to Sandy down by Queen. It seemed to me that Phillip's friends, if not Phillip himself, were bringing the hard stuff into the apartment. I decided to do what I always did when a cooling-off period was needed: go to Vancouver.

A strange opportunity had opened up along these lines. One of the regulars at Church Street the past year or so was a red-headed, bright-eyed and very eager young poet named Bill Howell (later a radio producer). To say the least, he didn't share the same aesthetic as the others in the group. He was down-home and folksy to a degree that most of us could scarcely warrant. He had an identical twin brother back in Nova Scotia and was forever going on about the wonderfully strange effects of being in that situation. He chattered constantly of the love of family and other concerns not all of us were familiar with in the same degree. I write of him here sheepishly, for after his first collection of poetry was published a few years later I was unconscionably rude to him in print (particularly, I seem to recall, because he had included a poem entitled "I Can't Wait to Get Home for Christmas and Be Hugged by Mom") and have been hoping to run into him ever since so that I might apologize.

Anyway, Howell had somehow come to know the concert artist Anton Kuerti, who had a special VW van remodelled to accommodate his favourite grand piano, so that he could take it with him wherever he performed. The vehicle had a kind of demi-lune-shaped dorsal fin on top; one tipped the instrument on its side and slid it on a track until it fit snugly between heavily padded bulkheads. Kuerti was playing in Vancouver, and would pay Bill and a companion to travel ahead with the rig, so that he could arrive later, by plane. Bill drove and got a few hundred dollars plus expenses, I rode shotgun and shared in the free food and lodging. An ideal arrangement except that I grew more frustrated with his almost criminal naiveté, as it then seemed to me to be, in those days when I wasn't exactly Vietnamese in my patience. It got so we couldn't stand the sound of each other's voices. As a result, I jumped out at Calgary, leaving him to negotiate the mountains by himself, and made my own way to Vancouver, where I knew how to get lost and wring the most benefit out of an urban monastic silence.

When I returned, Sandy Stagg had found Liz and Bill and the rest of us the perfect place to live, 52 Beverley Street, one of the Victorian terrace houses, steps from Queen. The rent (there was no lease) was $250, which was more than we were accustomed to paying, but then it was a big old place. Pat Lane had come back to town and he and Joe Rosenblatt, the dour but mocking poet and artist, author of *The LSD Leacock* and other contemporary classics, had helped the residents move in. People drew lots for rooms. I got one *in absentia*, and when I saw it for the first time, found it being slept in by Jim and Phillip and Jim's Swedish girlfriend, Annica, with traces of previous occupation by Erling Friis-Bastaad, another poet of that place and time (who subsequently moved to the Yukon). Bill took over the attic of the house and made it into a studio: the first he'd ever enjoyed.

With Sandy round the corner, it was now as if the two households were joined, though they were not precisely interchangeable. Sandy's chaos was different from ours. For the people at Beverley Street tended to be poets and musicians, particularly the musicians who played at the Global Village when, to take an example, there was a great benefit in aid of the *Harbinger*, an underground newspaper that had been busted. Our people also tended to be more politically active, demonstrating at the U.S. Consulate, for example. Sandy's place, by contrast, was theatrically inclined. It included a number of drag queens (one, named Murray, kept doing Sandy's hair in ever more outrageous ways) and many people who were involved with the Electric Circus on Queen Street East rather than with the Global Village. In fact, the entire resident dance company of the Circus lived at Sandy's for a while.

The actors in Sandy's circle made up some of the cast when the Global Village put on *Children of the Night*, whose *dramatis personae* was listed as a Queen, a

Straight Guy, the Bull Dyke, the Dirty Old Man, and
the Junkie. The last of these was supposed to be deaf-
and-dumb, which made it the perfect role for Yuri,
another member of Sandy's ménage, who spoke very little English and understood far less and was in real life
the sometimes boyfriend of the fellow playing the
Queen, for whom the part was not a stretch. The point
is that there was a new theatrical dimension to all our
lives, if only by association. Two doors away lived Marcel Horne, a professional fire-eater. He was a muscle-
bound fellow from Leamington, Ontario, whom Jim
Christy, the anarchist and adventurer, befriended.
Christy encouraged Marcel in the writing of his crude
autobiography, which he was then able to persuade
Peter Martin Associates to publish. *Annals of a Fire-
breather* was not always easy to take literally. It told of
Horne first running afoul of the law at seventeen, of
how he followed that course for a while (including one
arrest for bootlegging) and did nine months in solitary
before turning to the carnival for a livelihood. In time,
the account continued, he learned the physical and
mental skills of fire-eating from a gypsy in the New
Mexico desert. At one point, using the name Diablo, he
managed his own sideshow troupe, until his knife-
thrower missed and the blade slid into Marcel's chest.
Marcel enjoyed joint Swiss/Canadian citizenship—I've
forgotten how—and had more than one passport. At
one point, not too long before the Beverley Street days,
there was some story of his being jailed in Casablanca
with a homosexual leper but making good his escape to
Canada via Paris after the frontiers had been closed.
One never knew how much of this was true and will

never know now. He died a few years later in a car crash. Christy's friends tended to be of this order. Another of his heroes was a junkie and minor jazz musician named Charlie Leeds, whom he also encouraged to write—and got PMA to publish. A sad character. "Three days before his death," Christy would inform me later, "he had been down in Florida, trying to get a job as a caddy and reading Chaucer and Maupassant."

All this while there was anxious talk about finding Jim Byrnes and Phillip job offers so that they could become legal immigrants. Such offers were procured, but later, for reasons which time is obscuring from me now, they needed to find Canadian citizens to marry them. Liz had been romantically linked with Phillip, but I think it's fair to say that she was actually in pretty deep emotionally with Jim, as perhaps everyone but Jim himself could see. One night in March, the situation was made far stickier, and more dangerous, when Phillip turned up at Sandy's with the news that Jim and a young woman friend of Liz's had been busted for marijuana possession when the cops stopped Jim's car on Spadina Avenue. His companion was released on her own recognizance, I think, but Jim was being held pending bail. A collection was quickly taken up at the Global Village, and Liz and the others got the money together to spring him from the cells at 52 Division.

At that point, Phillip, whose stuff it probably was anyway, withdrew discreetly across the border but returned a week later to be a witness, along with Bill, when Liz and Jim were married in a Unitarian church, using a service I had written for the occasion (of which I now cannot recall a single word). By a nice coincidence, the nuptials were scheduled for the same day as the next episode in the marijuana case. The morning of the ceremony, Jim's co-defendant phoned Bill in a panic to say that matters had taken an unexpected turn for the worse in court. Instead of remanding the case, as the lawyer advised would be the usual procedure, the judge, noting Jim's record as a deserter, raised his bail to $1,000 and had him thrown into the Don Jail. Now Liz, Joe Nickell, any of us with a few dollars, had to cough it up. The wedding had to be postponed until the unfashionable hour of 5:30 p.m. The bridegroom wore a denim jacket he had stolen from the Don, with the name of the institution stencilled on the front and back. Phillip wore a purple bandanna and a full-length black cape. "It's difficult to say which freaked out the minister more," said Bill.

Jim and his co-defendant were in court again about ten days later, and it went smoothly: no more bail, and a remand. But a palpable fear hung over the proceedings. An Ontario judge wouldn't burden the taxpayer with the expense of sending Jim to jail for a long stretch. If convicted, Jim would be simply be deported back into the arms of the American military. Having escaped once, Lord knows when he might see light a second time.

The parties till 3:00 and 4:00, even 5:00 a.m., were still going on, yet people managed to get their work done somehow—I by making the now much longer trip to the CBC each night, Bill by retreating up to his studio, which he had decorated with a huge mural. But some people, the ones actually interested in new means of community, were becoming tired and sick.

"Some of the acid folk were still in various stages of high when I dragged my ass home this afternoon after a modelling job," Bill confided in me one day. "They all seem to want to keep up the drug thing. I'm soon going to be *very* paranoid." One night there were five uninvited all-night guests at our place alone, all very loud, and this was not a rare occurrence. The kitchen always overflowed with people. There was so much music it became just noise. You never knew who would be in which bed when you returned from a social outing, such as any performance by the Peoples' Revolutionary Band (a favourite group of the household's, with much more innovative musicianship than the name would suggest) or the Be-In held on the little lawn in front of Rochdale or, the following month, a demonstration at the U.S. Consulate with forty-seven arrested (a good turn-out). Bill wondered if he should try to play the role of tough cop (he wasn't sure if anyone would listen) or if he should just silently slip away and find another home (what a shame to leave his studio). In the end Liz was the one who assumed the tone of parental authority and gave notice to Jim (her legal husband), Annica (her legal husband's actual girlfriend), Phillip and his girlfriend, and a couple of others, literary people from the West, whose presence was actually my doing. Some begged extensions, some were miffed for a time, but generally the transition was handled effectively. This created room for a few more legitimate communards. Among these was the choreographer who gave dance lessons at the Global Village and to whom Bill had always been secretly attracted, in that gnomish way of his: too shy to talk without trying to be funny and self-deprecating, and so confining his lusts and thoughts to endless series of drawings.

The old decade had been over for months. It seemed as though something new should happen. There were a series of happy endings and some that were not so happy. Bill and the choreographer began living together and were a couple for five years, but Bill finally discovered to his certainty that he was intended to be happy with men, not women, and so moved in that direction, finding, I think, a lasting and rewarding relationship with a fine fellow. Because of the change he was eager to avoid his old friends, but after years of wearing him down with invitations, copies of new books and other gentle indications that he should look elsewhere for prejudice, that he was still my friend as I hoped I was still his, he came round, and we see each other frequently.

When the marijuana case finally came to trial, it proved anti-climactic. In a plea bargain the charges against Jim were dismissed and his co-defendant was fined only $200 on conviction. Phillip had simply disappeared back down the rabbit hole of America, and soon afterwards Jim relocated to the West Coast. One day not long after that, his old car ran out of gas on Vancouver Island. While Jim was pushing it up a mountain road, another driver, not seeing him round a curve, struck him a terrible blow. Both Jim's legs were amputated above the knee. Liz helped to nurse him back to health and to teach him to walk again. This was a great expression of love on Liz's part, but the two of them never lived together as husband and wife. Instead, Jim settled down to a stable home life with someone else, in Vancouver, and made his musical career all over again there, with the same rapturous success he'd had in Toronto. In the 1980s he became one of the stars of a U.S. television series, playing a handicapped character.

As for me, I was looking for roots which, in my innermost imagination, had already been planted for me long ago, for facts that had to do with my father and how I never really had the chance to benefit long enough from the love I knew he had for me. Our rents were due on the thirtieth of each month. After hearing the final outcome of Jim's court case on the eighteenth, I moved out of the house so as to avoid running into the next rent period and was determined to go to Montreal as soon as I could and there take ship for England.

I'd already missed the last CP liner, so I had to wait a few days until I could get a night train that would connect with a Russian ship bound for London. One of the people who had flitted in and out of first Church Street and then Beverley from the beginning had the small top floor of a house on the east side of Kendal Avenue in the Annex, a few steps from the Sibelius Park of Dennis Lee's wonderful poem. She offered to put me up for free until it was time for me to get to Union Station with my one Edwardian suit, my bag of essential books and a silver case of engraved calling cards. The arrangement was purely platonic. Indeed, I kept having to vacate the bed at odd hours so that she could frolic with a flutist named Claude (who later married the woman convicted in the marijuana case). But Bill didn't know this, nor did I know that he had secretly—in some of his most secret drawings—been lusting after her. As a result, he harboured needless jealousy of me, in his self-assigned role as the poor distant observer of all this activity of which he found himself in the middle. This too may have contributed to our being out of touch for a period later on.

Life was going to be much more productive and harmonious once I could get away for long enough to prepare myself properly to return. I had turned twenty-one, you see, and time was passing me by.